Workbook to Accompany

Computer Science with Pascal for Advanced Placement Students

Second Edition

Steven L. Mandell
Bowling Green State University

Colleen J. Mandell
Bowling Green State University

Susan Baumann

WEST PUBLISHING COMPANY
St. Paul   New York   Los Angeles   San Francisco

COPYRIGHT © 1989 by WEST PUBLISHING CO.
50 W. Kellogg Boulevard
P.O. Box 64526
St. Paul, MN 55164-1003

Printed in the United States of America
96 95 94 93 92 91   8 7 6 5 4 3 2 1
ISBN 0-314-51399-X

CONTENTS

INTRODUCTION

This workbook is to be used with the text *Computer Science with Pascal for Advanced Placement Students 2nd edition*. It is designed to assist the student in learning the text material and to give the student additional practice in writing and debugging Pascal programs. The following sections are included for each chapter: Chapter Objectives, Key Terms, Review of Key Terms, Multiple Choice Questions, Assignments (2).

In addition, the programming chapters (4 through 15) include Debugging Exercises (2) and Additional Programming Problems (2).

Chapter 1

Introduction to Computers and Computer Science

CHAPTER OBJECTIVES

After studying this chapter, you should be able to:

1. Explain the three functions of computers.
2. List the three things that make computers especially useful.
3. Define hardware and software.
4. Name the four basic types of computers and briefly describe each one.
5. Explain the three parts of a computer system.
6. Describe the purpose of such system programs as the supervisor program, the job control program, the input/output management system, language translation programs, library programs, and utility programs.
7. Discuss the three levels of computer programming languages.
8. Describe how a compiler works and how it differs from an interpreter.
9. Explain the concept of a structured programming language.
10. Give a brief history of the programming language Pascal.
11. Compare batch and interactive processing.

KEY TERMS

Application program A program written to meet a specific user need.

Arithmetic/logic unit (ALU) The component of the central processing unit that performs mathematical computations and logical operations.

Assembly language A programming language that uses symbolic names rather than the 0s and 1s of machine language; like machine language it is dependent upon the type of computer being used.

Auxiliary storage See **Secondary storage**.

1

Batch processing   Processing in which jobs are grouped together and processed in a continuous stream without user interaction.

Binary representation   See **Machine language**.

Block-structured language   Any programming language that encourages the writing of programs consisting of modules or blocks that work together to form a unified whole.

Central processing unit (CPU)   The "brain" of the computer; it is composed of two parts: the control unit and the arithmetic/logic unit.

Compiler   A language translation program that translates the entire source program into machine language before program execution begins.

Control unit   The part of the central processing unit that governs the actions of various components of the computer system.

Data   Facts that have been collected but not organized in a meaningful way.

Decision structure   A control structure used to determine whether a specific action will be taken.

Hard copy   Printed output.

Hardware   The physical components of a computer.

High-level language   Any programming language using English-like statements that must be translated into machine language before execution.

Information   Data that has been processed so that it is meaningful to the user.

Input   Data that is submitted to the computer so that the computer can process it.

Input/output (I/O) management system   A part of the operating system that controls and coordinates the CPU while receiving input, executing programs in storage, and regulating output.

Interactive processing   Processing in which the user is able to communicate directly with the computer during program execution.

Internal storage   See **Primary storage unit**.

Interpreter   A language translation program that translates each line of the source program into machine language and executes it before translating the next line.

Job control program   A program that translates into machine language the job control statements written by a programmer to indicate what the computer should do during program execution.

Language translation program   The instructions that translate a program written in assembly language or a high-level language into machine language.

Library program   A user-written or manufacturer-supplied program or subprogram that is used to perform a frequently needed task.

Loop A structure that allows a given section of a program to be repeated as many times as necessary.

Low-level language See **Assembly language**.

Machine language The only type of instructions that the computer is able to execute directly; it consists of combinations of 0s and 1s that represent on and off electrical states. Machine language is different for each type of computer.

Mainframe A large computer commonly used in business and industry.

Main memory See **Primary storage unit**.

Microcomputer The smallest and least expensive type of computer currently available; it is generally designed to be used by only one person at a time.

Minicomputer A computer with many of the capabilities of a mainframe, but generally lower priced and with a smaller primary storage unit.

Module See **Subprogram**.

Object program The executable instructions that are created when a source program is translated into machine language.

Operating system A collection of programs that permit a computer to manage itself and make efficient use of its resources.

Output The results of processing.

Primary memory See **Primary storage unit**.

Primary storage unit The component of a computer system that temporarily stores programs, data, and results.

Program A series of step-by-step instructions that the computer can use to solve a problem.

Secondary storage Memory that is used to supplement the primary storage unit. Since it is external to the computer, it takes longer to access than primary storage, but is less costly to provide.

Sequence A series of program statements that are executed in the order in which they are listed.

Soft copy Output displayed on a monitor screen.

Software A program or a collection of programs.

Source program A sequence of instructions, written in either assembly language or a high-level language, that is translated into machine language, resulting in an object program.

Subprogram A distinct part of a larger program, designed to perform a specific task. In structured programming, subprograms are used to make a program's logic easier to follow.

Supercomputer The largest, fastest computer currently available, capable of doing at least 10 million arithmetic operations per second.

Supervisor program The major component of an operating system; it coordinates the activities of all other parts of the operating system.

System program A program that facilitates efficient use of computer resources and aids in the development of application programs. System programs allocate storage space, direct input and output operations, manage files, and so forth.

Time-sharing system A system in which many terminals are connected to a central computer, which divides its time among the users.

Utility program A part of the operating system that can perform functions such as sorting, merging, and transferring data from one input or output device to another.

REVIEW OF KEY TERMS

The physical components of a computer system are referred to as _____

(1)

whereas the programs executed on the system are the _____. The three parts

(2)

of the computer system are the _____ which is the "brain" of the computer,

(3)

the _____ which temporarily stores programs and data, and _____

(4)   (5)

which allow programs and data to be input and output to the system. The _____

(6)

performs mathematical operations and makes comparisons. The CPU's _____

(7)

keeps the various parts of the system working together efficiently. Facts that have been collected

but are not meaningful are _____. When these facts have been processed to

(8)

give meaningful results, this is _____. Programs and their results can be

(9)

stored on _____ storage such as diskettes and tape. Output that is printed on

(10)

paper is _____ copy and output that is displayed on a monitor screen is

(11)

_____ copy. A small computer designed to be used by a single person is a(n)

(12)

_____. The fastest, most sophisticated computers available today are the

(13)

_____. _____ provide the ability to process large

(14)   (15)

quantities of data needed by business and industry. _____ are smaller than

(16)

mainframes and generally have smaller primary storage units but can often provide for the needs

of companies that do not need all of the capabilities of a mainframe. A series of instructions that

a computer can use to solve a problem is a(n) _____. Programs that are

(17)

written to direct the computer's internal operations are _____ programs
(18)

whereas programs that have been written to meet a specific need are _____
(19)

programs. A(n) _____ system consists of a series of system programs that is
(20)

designed to allow the computer to manage its resources efficiently. _____
(21)

language consists of 1s and 0s and is the only language that the computer can directly execute.

_____ languages contain English-like statements and are fairly independent of
(22)

the system being used. _____ languages are dependent on the system being
(23)

used but rather than the 1s and 0s of machine language they use symbolic names to represent

storage locations, mathematical operations, and so forth. Any programming problem can be

solved by using the needed combination of three structures: the _____ which
(24)

is a series of statements that are executed in the order in which they occur, the

_____ structure which determines whether a specific action will be taken, and
(25)

the _____ which allows a specific portion of a program to be executed
(26)

repeatedly. When _____ processing is used, the user can enter data and
(27)

obtain results during program execution whereas when using _____
(28)

processing it is necessary to submit all program data before execution starts. A(n)

_____ is a program that translates an entire _____ program
(29)   (30)

into a(n) _____ program which is then executed. A(n)
(31)

_____ translates and executes each statement of a program before proceeding
(32)

to the next statement.

MULTIPLE CHOICE

1. The study method referred to as SQ3R stands for (in the correct order) _____.
   a. Survey, Question, Read, Recite, and Review
   b. Study, Question, Read, Recite, and Review
   c. Survey, Question, Read, Review, Recite
   d. Study, Question, Read, Remember, Reread

2. When a computer calculates the amount of interest that is to be paid on a savings account, it is performing a(n) _____ operation.
   a. comparison
   b. storage
   c. arithmetic
   d. control

3. The computer system's display screen, disk drives, etc., make up its _____.
   a. operating system
   b. control unit
   c. software
   d. hardware

4. A disk drive is an example of a _____ that can store programs and program results so that they can be used by the computer system at a later time.
   a. peripheral device
   b. central processing unit
   c. system program
   d. primary storage unit

5. Facts that have been gathered, but not organized are _____ that can then be analyzed so that it is meaningful, resulting in _____.
   a. soft copy, hard copy
   b. software, hardware
   c. input, output
   d. data, information

6. Which of the following is not a reason for using system programs?
   a. They help the computer to use its resources efficiently.
   b. They eliminate the errors that can be made by human operators.
   c. They determine the order in which programs submitted to them will be executed.
   d. They automatically translate machine language programs into high-level language programs.

7. Which of the following is not a part of the operating system?
   a. supervisor program
   b. control unit
   c. input/output management system
   d. language translation program

8. Which of the following best describes the tasks performed by a supervisor program?
   a. It coordinates the activities of the other parts of the operating system.
   b. It coordinates the process of transferring programs, data, etc. from main memory to secondary storage.
   c. It translates high-level language programs into machine language.
   d. It performs arithmetic operations and logical comparisons.

9. A program that a school uses to generate and print report cards is a(n) _____ program.
   a. system
   b. hard copy
   c. supervisor
   d. application

10. A(n) _____ language program consists of a series of 1s and 0s that can be directly executed by a computer.
    a. assembly
    b. machine
    c. high-level
    d. structured

11. An advantage of using _____ instead of _____ is that this method uses less space in the computer's primary storage unit.
    a. a system program, an application program
    b. interactive processing, batch processing
    c. an interpreter, a compiler
    d. a source program, an object program

12. Which of the following is not a characteristic of structured programs?
    a. They have easy-to-follow logic.
    b. They are composed of the statements that use the needed combination of the three basic program structures.
    c. They are broken into subprograms, each designed to perform a specific task.
    d. They usually have more errors when they are first written than unstructured programs.

13. Which of the three basic types of program structures would be most appropriate to use when reading a list of 25 names?
    a. a loop
    b. a decision structure
    c. a control structure
    d. a sequence

14. Which of the three basic types of program structures would be most appropriate to use when determining if a specific test score deserves an A?
    a. a loop
    b. a decision structure
    c. a control structure
    d. a sequence

15. When the user enters data at the keyboard during program execution and gets seemingly immediate results on the display screen he or she is using _____.
    a. secondary storage
    b. interactive processing
    c. batch processing
    d. system programs

ASSIGNMENTS

Assignment 1

Complete the right column of the following table.

Operation	Type of Operation
A. Storing a program on magnetic tape.	
B. Totaling business income and expenses to determine the net profit.	
C. Arranging a list of names in alphabetical order.	
D. Sending an English report to the printer so that it can be printed on paper.	
E. Calculating a hockey player's statistics.	
F. Reading a list of city names and populations that have been entered at the keyboard.	
G. Examining the list in part F and determining the cities with the smallest and largest populations.	
H. Arranging the list in part F in order by population.	

Assignment 2

Fill in the following table with at least 5 different programs commonly contained in an operating system.

Program(s)	Purpose

Chapter 2

Programming Methodology

CHAPTER OBJECTIVES

After studying this chapter, you should be able to:

1. List the five steps in the programming process.
2. Explain what is meant by defining the problem.
3. Define the term algorithm.
4. Develop algorithms for simple problems.
5. Define top-down program design.
6. Explain how stepwise refinement is used in top-down programming.
7. Explain the difference between top-down and bottom-up program design.
8. List four advantages of top-down program design.
9. Draw flowcharts for simple problem solutions.
10. Write pseudocode for simple problem solutions.
11. Explain the terms debugging and testing.

KEY TERMS

Algorithm   The sequence of steps needed to solve a problem.

Bottom-up design   A method of problem solving that proceeds from the specific to the general.

Code   To write the solution to a programming problem in a programming language.

Debug   To locate and correct program errors.

Desk checking   A method of tracing through a program by hand in an attempt to locate any errors.

Double-alternative decision step   A decision step in which a specified action is taken if a condition is true; otherwise a different action is taken.

Flowchart   A graphic representation of the solution to a programming problem.

Programming process   The steps used to develop a solution to a programming problem.

Pseudocode   A description of a program's logic that is written using a combination of English words and words from a high-level language such as Pascal.

Semantics   A set of rules determining the meaning of a statement based on the relationship of words and symbols within the statement.

Single-alternative decision step   A decision step in which a specified action is taken if a condition is true; otherwise, execution passes on to the next statement.

Stepwise refinement   The process used in top-down design to break the steps needed for a problem solution into smaller and smaller subparts.

Structure chart   A diagram that visually illustrates how a problem solution has been divided into modules using stepwise refinement.

Syntax   The grammatical rules of a language.

Top-down design   A method of solving a problem by proceeding from the general to the specific.

REVIEW OF KEY TERMS

The _____ contains five steps that can be used to develop a solution to a
(1)

programming problem; this sequence of steps is an example of a(n) _____ .
(2)

_____ program design works from the general to the specific in developing a
(3)

solution; each step is broken into smaller and smaller substeps by using

_____ . _____ program design develops a solution by
(4)   (5)

working from the specific to the general. A(n) _____ shows how the
(6)

substeps in a problem solution are related to each other. _____ use symbols
(7)

to graphically depict the logic of a problem's solution whereas _____ depicts
(8)

the logic of the solution through the use of English words. In a(n) _____
(9)

decision step, a comparison is made; the result of the comparison determines whether a specified

action is taken. In a(n) _____ decision step, one action is taken if the
(10)

comparison is true and another if the comparison is false.

The process of writing a programming problem solution in a programming language is called

_____ . The grammatical rules of a programming language are its
(11)

_____ whereas the rules governing the meaning of the language's statements
(12)

are its _____ . Locating and correcting program errors is
(13)

_____ . When a programmer traces through a program by hand in an attempt
(14)

to locate any errors he or she is _____ the program.
(15)

MULTIPLE CHOICE

1. It is impossible to know what _____ will be needed by a program until the desired _____ has been determined.
   a. definitions, input
   b. input, output
   c. output, input
   d. information, data

2. Which of the following is not a characteristic of an algorithm?
   a. Each step must be clear and specific.
   b. The steps must be listed in the order in which they are to be carried out.
   c. There must be some result after the algorithm's steps are followed.
   d. The algorithm must be written in a programming language.

3. When you choose which topic to write about for Current Events class by first going to the library and determining what topics have the best (and most easily available) source material, you are practicing _____.
   a. algorithmic development
   b. structured programming
   c. bottom-up design
   d. top-down design

4. When you write a paper by first creating a general outline, then a more specific outline, fill in any missing details, and finally write the paper in prose form, you are practicing _____.
   a. algorithmic development
   b. structured programming
   c. bottom-up design
   d. top-down design

5. The following English statement contains a _____ error. The porgram ran perfectly.
   a. coding
   b. syntax
   c. semantics
   d. programming

6. The method by which the fourth step in the programming process is carried out will vary depending on _____.
   a. the type of input the computer needs
   b. how the programming problem has been documented
   c. how the programming problem has been defined
   d. the computer system being used

7. Which of the following is the flowchart symbol for an input/output step?
   a.

   b.

   c.

   d.

8. Which of the following flowcharts could be used to determine if an angle is acute, right, or obtuse?

a.
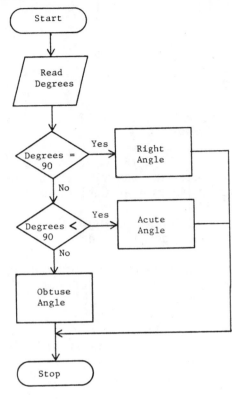

c.
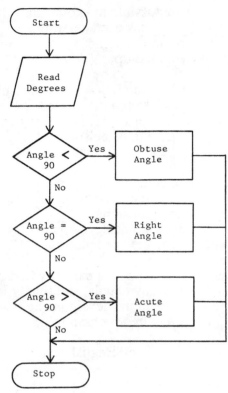

b.
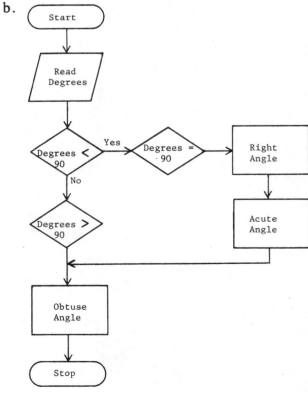

d.
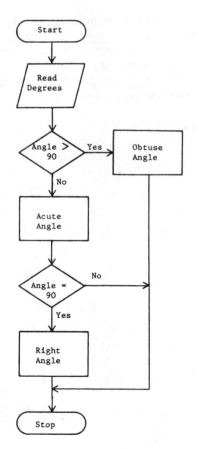

9. It is important that programs be run with a wide variety of data because _____.
    a. doing so makes the logic of the program easier to understand
    b. it makes the program execute more quickly
    c. a program may obtain correct results sometimes and incorrect results other times
    d. it makes coding the program easier

Use the following flowchart to answer Questions 10-13.

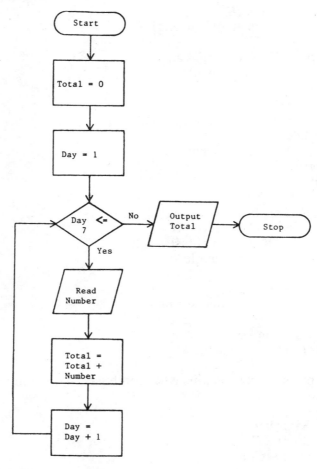

10. The purpose of the statement "Total = 0" is to _____.
    a. start the program
    b. determine the sum of the numbers read
    c. initialize Total to zero
    d. print the value of Total at the end of the program

11. How many times will the decision step in the flowchart be executed?
    a. 1 time   c. 7 times
    b. 6 times   d. 8 times

12. How many times will the Read Number step be executed?
    a. 8 times   c. 6 times
    b. 7 times   d. 1 time

13. The loop in this flowchart will be executed as long as _____.
    a. Day is less than or equal to 7
    b. Day is greater than 7
    c. Total is equal to 0
    d. Number is less than or equal to 7

14. Which of the following segments of pseudocode could be used to determine if an angle is acute, right, or obtuse?
    a. Read Angle
       If Angle is greater than 90
          Then print "This is an obtuse angle."
          Else if Angle = 90
             Then print "This is a right angle."
             Else print "This is an acute angle."
    b. Read Angle
       If Angle less than 90
          Then print "This is an obtuse angle."
          Else if Angle = 90
             Then print "This is a right angle."
             Else print "This is an acute angle."
    c. Read Angle
       If Angle less than 90
          Then print "This is an acute angle."
          Else if Angle is not equal to 90
             Then print "This is an obtuse angle."
             Print "This is a right angle."
    d. Read Angle
       If Angle is not equal to 90
          Then print "This is an obtuse angle."
          Else print "This angle is a right angle."
       If Angle is less than 90
          Then print "This is an acute angle."

15. The following pseudocode contains what combination of structures?
       While Count <= 7 do
          Read Day
          If Day = Saturday
             Then Count = 7
             Else Count = Count + 1
       End (* Loop *)
    a. sequence, loop
    b. sequence, single-alternative decision structure
    c. loop, single-alternative decision structure
    d. loop, double-alternative decision structure

ASSIGNMENTS

Assignment 1

Draw a structure for an activity you have performed. Use at least three levels.

Assignment 2

Draw a flowchart for an activity that contains a double-alternative decision structure. Draw a second flowchart that contains a single-alternative decision structure. Write the corresponding pseudocode for each structure.

Chapter 3

Introduction to Pascal

CHAPTER OBJECTIVES

After studying this chapter, you should be able to:

1. Create valid Pascal identifiers.
2. Describe the difference between a program variable and a program constant.
3. Write valid program headings, variable declaration statements, and constant definition statements.
4. Identify the four simple data types discussed in this chapter and describe the characteristics of each.
5. Identify the basic parts of a Pascal program.
6. Be able to use the semicolon properly in a Pascal program.
7. Assign values to variables.
8. Perform mathematical operations on variables and constants.
9. Explain the operator precedence rules and use them properly in evaluating mathematical expressions.
10. Convert standard mathematical formulas into their Pascal equivalents.

KEY TERMS

Arithmetic operator   An operator that represents a mathematical operation such as addition or division.

Assignment-compatible   If a value, expression, or variable can be assigned to a variable without error, it is said to be assignment-compatible.

Assignment operator   A symbol (:=) that causes the value of the expression to the right of the symbol to be assigned to the variable to the left.

Assignment statement   A statement that assigns a value to a specific variable.

Comment   A nonexecutable statement that explains the program to humans. In Pascal, comments must be enclosed in parentheses and asterisks (* like this *) or in braces {like this}.

Constant   A value that does not change during program execution.

Decimal notation   A method of representing a real number with at least one digit before and one digit after the decimal point.

Declaration section   The part of a Pascal program that states the constants, variables, and so on that the program will use.

Documentation   The use of comments within a program or external written materials to explain the action of a program to humans.

Exponential notation   Expressing a number by using powers of ten. For example, 63410.0 would be represented in exponential notation as 6.341E+4.

Identifier   A symbolic name used to represent an object in a program.

Operator precedence rules   Conventions that govern the order in which operators are evaluated.

Program body   The part of a program containing executable statements. This is where the actual work of the program is done. It is enclosed within a *begin-end* pair followed by a period.

Program heading   The first line of a Pascal program. It consists of three parts: the reserved identifier **program**, the name of the program, and the files used by the program.

Reserved identifier   A word having a predefined meaning to the compiler. It cannot be redefined by the programmer.

Standard identifier   A word having a predefined meaning to the compiler. It can be redefined by the programmer, although this is poor programming practice.

User-defined identifier   An identifier that is defined by the programmer.

Variable   A storage location containing a value that may change during program execution. Variables have three characteristics: a name, a value, and a type.

REVIEW OF KEY TERMS

A Pascal _____ must start with a letter and consist of a combination of
(1)

letters and digits. _____ have predefined meanings to the compiler and cannot
(2)

be redefined by the programmer. _____ also have predefined meanings but
(3)

can be redefined by the programmer. A(n) _____ is a storage location that
(4)

can be assigned a value that changes during program execution. The value of a(n)

_____, on the other hand, cannot be changed during program execution. The
(5)

most common method of representing a real number is by using _____
(6)

notation. Using _____ notation involves using a value called the
(7)

_____ which is multiplied by 10 to the specified power, called the
(8)

_____. The first statement in a program is the _____ and
(9)   (10)

identifies the program. This statement is followed by the _____ which
(11)

declares any constants, variables, and so forth that are used by the program. The program

_____ contains the part of the program that performs the work.
(12)

_____ are placed in a program to explain the program to humans; the compiler
(13)

skips over them. Values can be assigned to variables by using _____
(14)

statements. The _____ is represented by the symbol ':='. The symbols +, -,
(15)

*, and / are examples of _____. In a mathematical expression, the
(16)

_____ are used to determine the order in which the operators will be
(17)

evaluated. The number 7 can be assigned to a real variable because integer values and real

variables are _____.

(18)

MULTIPLE CHOICE

1. Which of the following is not a valid Pascal identifier?
    - a. 4th
    - b. Gone
    - c. SomeDay
    - d. TotalBalance

2. Why cannot the word *end* be used as a variable name?
    - a. It does not start with a number.
    - b. It has too few letters.
    - c. It does not contain any digits.
    - d. It is a reserved word.

3. Which of the following is not a category of identifiers?
    - a. reserved identifiers
    - b. data types
    - c. user-defined identifiers
    - d. standard identifiers

4. Which of the following is not a valid integer?
    - a. -100
    - b. $250
    - c. +8
    - d. 0

5. The real number 3967.82 can be represented in exponential notation as _____.
    - a. 3.96782E+3
    - b. 0.396782E+2
    - c. 3.96782E+2
    - d. 39.6782E+3

6. Which of the following is *not* a standard data type in Standard Pascal?
    - a. Real
    - b. Integer
    - c. String
    - d. Boolean

7. Which of the following is *not* contained in a program heading?
    - a. The name of the program.
    - b. The reserved word *program*.
    - c. The external files used by the program.
    - d. The names of the variables used by the program.

8. What is placed at the end of a program?
    - a. The word *end* followed by a semicolon.
    - b. The word *end* followed by a period.
    - c. The word *stop* followed by a period.
    - d. The word *finished* followed by a period.

9. Suppose you need to declare a constant *pi* which should be set equal to 3.1416 and two variables. *Radius* and *Circumference* both of type *real*. Which of the following program segments will do this?

    - a. ```
      const
          pi = 3.1416;

      var
          Radius, Circumference : real;
      ```
    - b.  ```
      const
          pi := 3.1416;

      var
          Radius, Circumference : real;
      ```
    - c. ```
      const
          pi = 3.1416;
          Radius, Circumference : real;
      ```
    - d.  ```
      const
          pi = 3.1416;

      var
          Radius, Circumference = real;
      ```

10. Which of the following statements will assign the value 'A' to the *char* variable *Alphabet*?
    a. Alphabet = 'A'
    b. Alphabet := 'A'
    c. A is assigned to Alphabet
    d. A := Alphabet

11. Which of the following is *not* a Pascal arithmetic operator?
    a. X
    b. +
    c. *
    d. /

12. Which of the following expressions evaluates as 14?
    a. 6 - 2 * 4
    b. 17 div (4 * 1) + 10
    c. 32 - 4 / 2
    d. 68 mod 10 * 2 - 2

13. Which of the following lists the order in which arithmetic expressions are evaluated?
    a. 1. parenthesized expressions
        2. *, /, div, mod
        3. +, -
    b. 1. parenthesized expressions
        2. +, -
        3. *, /, div, mod
    c. 1. *, /, div, mod
        2. +, -
        3. parenthesized expressions
    d. 1. +, -
        2. *, /, div, mod
        3. parenthesized expressions

14. The expression 58 div 14 + 20 / 4 equals _____.
    a. 9
    b. 6
    c. 3
    d. 24

15. Which statement below is a correct Pascal translation of the following formula?

$$\frac{8 + 4^3}{8} - 17 \times 2 + 3$$

    a. 8 + 4 * 4 * 4 / 8 - 17 * 2 + 3
    b. (8 + 4 * 4 * 4) / 8 - 17 * 2 + 3
    c. 8 + 4 * 4 * 4 / 8 - (17 * 2 + 3)
    d. (8 + 4 * 4 * 4) / 8 - (17 * 2 + 3)

ASSIGNMENTS

Assignment 1

Identify the following program segments as either valid or invalid. If invalid, give the reason(s).

Program Segment	Valid? (Y/N)	If Invalid Why?
1. program Read (input, output);		
2. program DetermineHeight (input, output);		
3. program Volume (input, output),		

4. const
        Percentage1 := 0.07;
        Percentage2 := 0.095;		

5. const
        PossiblePoints = 80;
 	
    var
        StudentScore : integer;
 	
    begin
        StudentScore := 75.5		

6. var
        SqFeet : real;
 	
    begin
        SqFeet := 0;
        SqFeet := 10 + SqFeet		

7. var Distance : real, Height : integer;		

Assignment 2

Use the following program segment to fill in the right column of the table below (assume that each numbered section is independent of values assigned to variables in the previous sections):

```
const
    LargeNum  =  14.5;
    MedNum    =  10;
    SmallNum  =  5.25;
    Symbol    =  '%';

var
    N1, N2  :  real;
    I1, I2, :  integer;
    C1      :  char;
```

1. N1 := 12.5 + 5.25	N1 =
2. I2 := 44 + MedNum div 12	I2 =
3. N1 := LargeNum * 3 + 18	N1 =
4. N1 := 77 mod 18 / 6 + 2	N1 =
5. I2 := 44 * 2 mod MedNum	I2 =
6. C1 := Symbol	C1 =
7. N2 := 17.6; N1 := 2 * (N2 - 18)	N1 =
8. N1 := 14 - 18.4 / (4 mod 5)	N1 =
9. I1 := 14; I1 := 82 + I1 * 3	I1 =
10. N1 := SmallNum - 2.5 / 4	N1 =

Chapter 4

Input/Output and Procedures

CHAPTER OBJECTIVES

After studying this chapter, you should be able to:

1. Explain the purpose of the *write* and *writeln* statements.
2. Explain the difference between the *write* and *writeln* statements when writing to the screen.
3. Use the *write* and *writeln* statements to display prompts on the screen.
4. Use the *write* and *writeln* statements to display program results on the screen.
5. Explain the purpose of the *read* and *readln* statements.
6. Explain the difference between the *read* and *readln* statements when reading data input at the keyboard.
7. Use the *read* and *readln* statements to read data that has been entered at the keyboard.
8. Format the output of real numbers and integers.
9. Format character string output.
10. Define and give examples of standard procedures.
11. Divide programming problems by task into procedures.
12. Explain how parameters are used to pass values to and from procedures.
13. Write simple procedures and procedure calls.
14. Explain the difference between variable parameters and value parameters.

KEY TERMS

Actual parameter   A value (a variable, expression, or constant) that is passed to a procedure or function when it is called, and is manipulated by the procedure or function. It is substituted for its corresponding formal parameter.

Argument   See **Actual parameter**.

Built-in procedure   See **Standard procedure**.

Character string   A literal enclosed in single quotes, frequently used to label output or as a prompt.

Field-width parameter   A value used to control the position of data within a fixed output field.

Formal parameter   An identifier listed in a procedure declaration and used to represent a value that will be passed to the procedure by the calling program through an actual parameter.

Format   To control the physical arrangement of output.

Global variable   A variable declared in the main program; it may be referred to anywhere in the program.

Literal   An expression consisting of alphabetic, numeric, or special characters, or any combination of the three, and representing only those characters; it is not a symbol for any other value.

Local variable   A variable declared in a subprogram; it is undefined outside of that subprogram.

Procedure   A subprogram that performs a specific task.

Prompt   A statement displayed on the monitor screen that instructs the user to enter data.

Right-justified   Output placed so that the last character is at the right margin of the output field.

Standard procedure   A procedure that is built into the Pascal language. To use the procedure, the programmer simply includes its name in a procedure call.

User-defined procedure   A procedure that the programmer writes to perform a specific task. User-defined procedures are used to modularize programs and consist of a procedure heading, declaration section, and a body.

Value parameter   A parameter (in a procedure), the value of which is copied into a local variable. Any changes made to the value are not passed back to the calling program.

Variable parameter   A parameter (in a procedure), the value of which is returned to the calling program. It must be preceded by the reserved identifier *var* in the formal parameter list.

REVIEW OF KEY TERMS

When the programmer wishes the user to enter data, a(n) _____ (1) should

be displayed indicating the type and quantity of data needed. Constant values, such as numbers

and character strings, are _____ (2) . The literal 'Sis Hesse' is also a(n)

_____ (3) . Controlling the manner in which output is displayed is

_____ (4) . The integer value representing the size of a fixed field in which output

is to be placed is a(n) _____ (5) parameter. When output is formatted so that the

last character is at the right margin of the field, it is _____ (6) . A(n)

_____ (7) procedure is built into the Pascal compiler whereas a(n)

_____ (8) procedure is written by the programmer. _____ (9)

parameters (or _____ (10)) are used to pass values to procedures. When the

procedure is called, these parameters are substituted for the _____ (11) parameters

in the procedure heading. A variable that is defined in the main program is

_____ (12) and can be used anywhere in the program. A variable that is defined in

a particular procedure is _____ (13) to that procedure and cannot be used

elsewhere. _____ (14) parameters do not return their values to the calling program

whereas _____ (15) parameters do.

MULTIPLE CHOICE

1. A _____ can be any combination of alphabetic, numeric, or special characters.
   a. parameter
   b. literal
   c. variable
   d. procedure

2. Character strings must be enclosed in _____.
   a. double quotes
   b. single quotes
   c. parentheses
   d. brackets

3. A _____ statement causes a carriage return to be executed whereas a _____ does not.
   a. prompt, write
   b. output, writeln
   c. writeln, write
   d. write, writeln

4. What will the output of the following statement look like?
       writeln ('Flight':12, 'Destination':14, 'Time':8)
   a. FlightDestinationTime
   b.   Flight   Destination   Time
   c. Flight   Destination   Time
   d.   'Flight' 'Destination' 'Time'

5. What will be output by the following statement?
       writeln ('Jack jumped over the candlestick.':12)
   a. Jack jumped over the candlestick.
   b.   Jack jumped over the candlestick.
   c. Jack jumped
   d.   Jack jumped

6. If the input is arranged as follows:
       8   7   1
       2
       6
   what values will the integer variables I1, I2, and I3 have after these *readln* statements are executed?
       readln (I1, I2);
       readln;
       readln (I3)
   a. 8, 7, 2
   b. 8, 2, 6
   c. 8, 7, 6
   d. 8, 7, 1

7. Standard procedures are _____ whereas user-defined procedures are _____.
   a. included in the compiler, written by the programmer
   b. global, local
   c. local, global
   d. written by the programmer, included in the compiler

8. Which of the following is *not* a standard procedure?
   a. writeln
   b. read
   c. write
   d. const

9. Actual parameters are also called _____.
   a. formal parameters
   b. procedures
   c. arguments
   d. global variables

Use the following program segment to answer Questions 10-13.

```
program FindPay (input, output);

var
    Hours, TaxRate, NetPay : real;
    PayCode : char;

procedure Calculate (Hours, TaxRate : real; PayCode : char;
                     var NetPay : real);

var
    GrossPay : real;

begin   (* Calculate *)

    If PayCode = 'A'
       then GrossPay := Hours * 4.80
       else if PayCode = 'B'
               then GrossPay := Hours * 5.24
               else GrossPay := Hours * 6.08;
    Netpay := (GrossPay - GrossPay * TaxRate)

end;    (* Calculate *)

begin    (* main *)

    write ('Enter the pay code (A, B, or C): ');
    readln (PayCode);
    write ('Enter hours worked: ');
    readln (Hours);
    write ('Enter the tax rate: ');
    readln (TaxRate);

    Calculate (Hours, TaxRate, PayCode, NetPay);

    writeln ('The net pay is ', NetPay:9:2)

end.    (* main *)
```

10. Procedure *Calculate* has _____ value parameter(s) and _____ variable parameter(s).
    a. 3, 1
    b. 4, 0
    c. 1, 3
    d. 0, 4

11. The variable *GrossPay* is a(n) _____.
    a. global variable
    b. formal parameter
    c. argument
    d. local variable

12. Why is the following an invalid procedure call to procedure *Calculate*?
    Calculate (42, 18.5, 'B', 429.24)
    a. The first actual parameter must be a real number rather than an integer.
    b. The fourth actual parameter is a variable parameter and therefore must be a variable and not a literal.
    c. The third actual parameter must be a real number rather than a character value.
    d. The reserved word *procedure* is missing.

13. Which of the following is a valid procedure call for procedure *Calculate*?
    a. procedure Calculate (38.5, 12.25, 'C', GrossPay)
    b. Calculate (38.5, 18.4, 'B', TotalPay)
    c. Calculate (40, 15.5, A, GrossPay)
    d. Calculate (40, 'C', GrossPay)

14. _____ parameters return their values to the calling program whereas _____ parameters do not.
    a. Variable, value   c. Formal, local
    b. Value, variable   d. Local, global

15. Actual parameters are substituted for formal parameters based on _____.
    a. their types
    b. their respective positions in the parameter lists
    c. the values they contain
    d. the purpose of the procedure

ASSIGNMENTS

Assignment 1

Fill in the right column of the table below. Use the following declarations in evaluating the values of the variables.

```
var
    R1, R2, R3, R4 : real;
    I1, I2 : integer;
    C1, C2, C3, C4 : char;
```

Input

```
14.5   7.2   8.0
9.1   2.3
0.0
1.8   7.5
36.5   8.1   19.2
```

Statements

Statement				
readln (R1, R2);	R1 = ____	R2 = ____		
read (R3, R1);	R1 = ____	R2 = ____	R3 = ____	
readln (R4);	R1 = ____	R2 = ____	R3 = ____	R4 = ____
read (R2, R4);	R1 = ____	R2 = ____	R3 = ____	R4 = ____
read (R1);	R1 = ____	R2 = ____	R3 = ____	R4 = ____
readln (R3)	R1 = ____	R2 = ____	R3 = ____	R4 = ____

Input

```
MON  8  1  14  L
PAB9  17  42
VINE
SRW
SPRING
WINTER
```

Statements

Statement				
read (C1, C3);	C1 = ____	C3 = ____		
read (C4, I1);	C1 = ____	C3 = ____	C4 = ____	I1 = ____
readln (I2);	C1 = ____	C3 = ____	C4 = ____	I2 = ____
readln (C1, C2);	C1 = ____	C2 = ____	C3 = ____	C4 = ____
read (C4);	C1 = ____	C2 = ____	C3 = ____	C4 = ____
readln (C1, C2, C4);	C1 = ____	C2 = ____	C3 = ____	C4 = ____
read (C4);	C1 = ____	C2 = ____	C3 = ____	C4 = ____
readln (C2)	C1 = ____	C2 = ____	C3 = ____	C4 = ____

Assignment 2

Use the program below to fill in the values of the variables listed in the table.


```
program TestValues (input, output);

var
    Area1, Area2, TotalArea, WindowArea, DoorArea, Paint : real;
    NumDoors, NumWindows : integer;

(*************************************************************************)

procedure SubtractWindows (TotalArea : real; var WindowArea : real;
                           var NumWindows : integer);

var
   LargeWindows, SmallWindows : integer;

begin   (* SubtractWindows *)

   LargeWindows := 4;
   SmallWindows := 6;
   NumWindows := LargeWindows + SmallWindows;
   WindowArea := (LargeWindows * 5 + SmallWindows * 3);
1. TotalArea := TotalArea - WindowArea

end;   (* SubtractWindows *)

(*************************************************************************)

procedure  SubtractDoors (var TotalArea, DoorArea : real; NumDoors :
                          integer);

begin   (* SubtractDoors *)

   NumDoors := 2;
   DoorArea := NumDoors * 6;
2. TotalArea := TotalArea - DoorArea

end;   (* SubtractDoors *)

(*************************************************************************)

begin   (* main *)

   Area1 := 200;
   Area2 := 400;
   TotalArea := Area1 + Area2;
   SubtractWindows (TotalArea, WindowArea, NumWindows);
   SubtractDoors (TotalArea, DoorArea, NumDoors);
   writeln ('The number of windows is ', NumWindows:4);
   writeln ('The number of doors is ', NumDoors:4);
   Paint := TotalArea / 450;
3. writeln ('The amount of paint needed is ', Paint:8:2, ' gallons.')

end.   (* main *)
```

Assignment 2 (cont.)

Location #1 (end of first procedure)		Location #2 (end of second procedure)		Location #3 (end of main program)	
Variable	**Value**	**Variable**	**Value**	**Variable**	**Value**
LargeWindows		NumDoors		Area1	
SmallWindows		DoorArea		Area2	
NumWindows		TotalArea		TotalArea	
WindowArea				WindowArea	
TotalArea				DoorArea	
				Paint	
				NumDoors	
				NumWindows	

DEBUGGING EXERCISES

Identify and correct the errors in the following program segments.

Use the following declarations for exercises 1-4:

```
program WeightConversion (input, output);
const
    KiloPerPound = 0.45359;
var
    KiloWeight, PoundWeight, Weight : real;
    IdNumber : integer;
```

1. KiloPerPound := 0.45359

2. KiloWeight := PoundWeight x KiloPerPound

3. writeln ('Idnumber', 'Height', 'Weight(P)', 'Weight(K)');
    writeln (IdNumber:10, Height:5:2, KiloWeight:7:2, PoundWeight:7:2)

4. writeln ('Enter', IdNumber, Height, PoundWeight)

PROGRAMMING PROBLEMS

1.   Write a program that will help an art student determine the cost of framing artwork. The program should prompt the student for the length and the width of the item. Then the amount of glass needed (in square inches) and the cost of the glass should be determined. Assume the glass costs 2 cents a square inch. Next the cost of the framing material should be determined. The wood used for framing is 1-inch wide pine and costs $1.45 a foot. Use procedures as appropriate.

2.   The pressure that a dry gas exerts on its container is directly proportional to the atmospheric temperature (in degrees Kelvin). The formula can be stated as follows:

$$\frac{Pressure1}{Temp1} = \frac{Pressure2}{Temp2}$$

where Pressure1 is the original pressure, Temp1 is the original Kelvin temperature, Pressure2 is the new pressure and Temp2 is the new Kelvin temperature.
     Write a program that will prompt the user to enter the amount of pressure in his or her tires (in pounds per square inch) at a specific Celsius temperature. The program should display a table listing the tire pressure at the following Celsius temperatures: -10, 0, 10, 20, and 30. It will be necessary to convert the Celsius temperatures to Kelvin before determining the new pressure. Use the formula: Kelvin Temperature = Celsius Temperature + 273.

Chapter 5

Decision Structures

CHAPTER OBJECTIVES

After studying this chapter, you should be able to:

1. Give a definition for each of the two types of control statements.
2. Explain how the *if/then* and *if/then/else* statements are used to control the flow of program execution.
3. Use the *if/then* and *if/then/else* statements in programs.
4. Explain the meaning of each of the relational operators.
5. Write compound statements.
6. Explain how nested *if/then/else* statements work.
7. Write nested *if/then/else* statements.
8. Write *case* statements.
9. Evaluate expressions containing Boolean operators.
10. Write statements containing Boolean operators.

KEY TERMS

Boolean operator   An operator that is used to combine two expressions with the resulting expression being either true or false. In Standard Pascal, the Boolean operators are *not*, *and*, and *or*.

Collating sequence   The internal ordering that the computer assigns to the characters it is able to recognize. This ordering allows the computer to make comparisons between different character values.

Control statement   A statement used to determine the order in which program statements will be executed. Decision statements and looping statements are the two types of control statements.

Nesting   The process of enclosing one control structure within another, as with an *if* statement that is embedded within another *if* statement.

Ordinal data type A data type in which each possible value (except the first) has a unique predecessor, and each possible value (except the last) has a unique successor.

Relational operator An operator that is used to compare two operands. In Standard Pascal, the relational operators are <, <=, =, >=, >, < >.

REVIEW OF KEY TERMS

_____ statements allow the programmer to alter the order in which
(1)

statements are executed. The process of placing one of these statements inside another is called

_____. When comparing one operand with another _____
(2)   (3)

operators are used. The computer uses its _____ sequence to determine if one
(4)

character value is greater than another. In _____ data types any value in that
(5)

type (except the first) must have a unique successor. The expression "(5 < > Y) or (Y >= 10)" is

an example of a(n) _____ expression.
(6)

MULTIPLE CHOICE

1. A control statement can be used to _____.
    a. call a procedure
    b. assign a value to a variable
    c. alter the normal flow of program execution
    d. perform arithmetic operations

2. The two types of control statements are _____.
    a. procedure headings and procedure calls   c. sequence statements and loops
    b. arithmetic and logical statements   d. decision statements and loops

3. The correct format for the double-alternative *if* statement is _____.
    a. if condition   c. if condition
           then statement1   then statement1;
           else statement2   else statement2
    b. if condition   d. if statement
           then statement   then condition1
                                               else condition2

4. When a relational operator is used in an expression, the expression must evaluate as a(n) _____.
    a. integer   c. real number
    b. character value   d. Boolean value (true or false)

5. Which of the following is *not* a relational operator?
    a. < >   c. >=
    b. :=   d. =

Use the following program segment to answer Questions 6-9. Assume that *Quantity* is of type *integer* and *Price* and *PerItem* are of type *real*.

```
if Quantity > 25
   then Price := PerItem * Quantity * 0.80
   else if Quantity > 10
           then Price := PerItem * Quantity * 0.90
           else Price := PerItem * Quantity
```

6. Which of the following is a true statement about this program segment?
    a. It contains an *if/then/else* statement with an *if/then/else* statement nested in its *else* clause.
    b. It contains an *if/then/else* statement with an *if/then/else* statement nested in its *then* clause.
    c. It contains two *if/then/else* statements which are not nested.
    d. It contains three nested *if/then/else* statements.

7. The first relational operator in this statement is _____.
    a. Quantity   c. :=
    b. Price   d. >

8. If the value of *Quantity* is 10 and *PerItem* is 5.50, what value will be assigned to *Price*?
    a. 5.50   c. 55.00
    b. 49.50   d. 44.00

9. If the value of **Quantity** is 21 and **PerItem** is 5.50, what value will be assigned to **Price**?
   a. 115.50
   b. 103.95
   c. 92.40
   d. 11.00

10. A(n) _____ is used to denote a compound statement.
    a. *if/then/else* statement
    b. loop
    c. decision statement
    d. *begin-end* pair

11. Which of the following is true concerning the *case* statement?
    a. It can be used to check for a range of real numbers.
    b. The labels can be any standard data type.
    c. The *begin* and *end* marking its limits are optional.
    d. While it has no *begin*, an *end* is required.

Use the following program segment to answer Questions 12-15.

```
case Class of
    108 : Room := 214;
    224 : Room := 31;
    165 : Room := 100;
    217 : Room := 122;
    189 : Room := 85
end   (* case *)
```

12. In this example the *case* selector is _____.
    a. Class
    b. Room
    c. the reserved word *case*
    d. There is no *case* selector.

13. *Class* must be of data type _____ and *Room* must be of data type _____.
    a. char, char
    b. selector, integer
    c. real, real
    d. integer, integer

14. The label(s) in this example is/are _____.
    a. Class
    b. 108, 224, 165, 217, 189
    c. 214, 31, 100, 122, 85
    d. Room

15. If the value of **Class** were 165 when this **case** statement was executed, what would happen?
    a. A run-time error would occur.
    b. The body of the *case* statement would not be executed.
    c. The value 100 would be assigned to **Room**.
    d. The value 100 would be assigned to **Class**.

16. Which of the following is *not* a Boolean operator?
    a. not
    b. and
    c. =
    d. or

17. Which of the expressions below evaluates as false?
    a. (14 > 12) and (10 = 9 + 1)
    b. (14 > 12) or (10 = 9 + 1)
    c. not (18 <= 18) or (17 * 2 = 34)
    d. (72 / 8) > 8) and not (18 = 18)

ASSIGNMENTS

Assignment 1

Evaluate the expressions listed in the following table as true or false.

Expression	True or False
1. 8 + 15 mod 3 > 6	
2. (67 - 15 = 52) and not (88 < > 77)	
3. (77 <= 18 / 6 + 75) or (11 + 2 mod 2 = 1)	
4. 19 + 7 div 1 + 9 = 35	
5. 10 / 2 + 8.7 * 2 <= 22	
6. (8 - 4 * 3 < > 4) and (24 / 6 + 3 = 7)	
7. not (88 + 12 div 2 = 94) or (19 - 1 >= 18)	

Assignment 2

Write the program segments to implement the following flowcharts:

a.

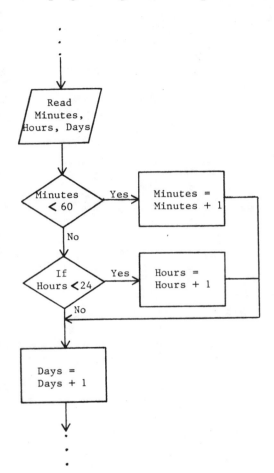

b.

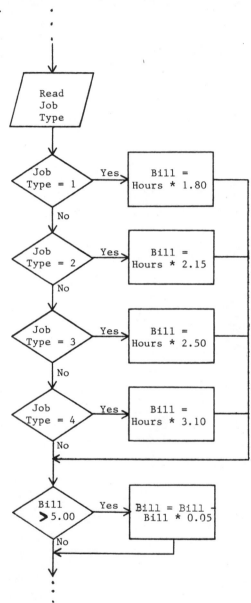

DEBUGGING EXERCISES

Identify and correct the errors in the following program or program segments.

Use the following program segment to answer debugging exercises 1 and 2:

```
program Computation (input, output);

var
    Temp, x, y : real;
    a, b : integer;

begin   (* Computation *)

    x := 2 + 2;
    y := 6;
    Temp := 4;
    a := 7;
    b := 2 * 4
```

1. If Temp = x
```
    then b := a div 2
    else b := a mod 3.5
```

2. If Temp > 0
```
    then x := a div b
    else b := y / x
```

3. program Play (input, output);
```
    var
        Move, Win : integer;

    procedure Game (Move : integer; var Win : boolean);

    begin   (* Game *)

        If Move > 8
            then Win = true
            else Win = false

    end;   (* Game *)

    begin   (* main *)

        Game (Move, Win)

    end.   (* main *)
```

PROGRAMMING PROBLEMS

1. Write a five-question multiple choice test based on this chapter. Call a procedure to display each question. Prompt the user to enter an answer. The program should then display a message stating whether the answer was correct. At the end of the program, display the total number of correct answers.

2. The football coach would like a program to determine if a given student is a likely candidate for the high school football team. The coach feels that students should meet the following criteria to be candidates:

1. Male
2. Weigh more than 130 pounds
3. Be taller than 5' 8"
4. Have a grade point average of at least 2.5

Write a program that will allow the coach to enter the above data to determine whether the student is a likely candidate.

Chapter 6

Loops

CHAPTER OBJECTIVES

After studying this chapter, you should be able to:

1. Use *while/do* loops in programs when appropriate.
2. Use *repeat/until* loops in programs when appropriate.
3. Use *for* loops in programs when appropriate.
4. Compare the three types of loop statements.
5. Give a definition of a counting loop.
6. Explain how Boolean flags are used to control loops.
7. Explain how sentinel values are used to control loops.
8. Write programs that contain counting loops.
9. Write loops that are controlled by Boolean flags and sentinel values.

KEY TERMS

Counting loop   A loop that is executed a stated number of times. The number of repetitions to be executed must be determined before the loop is entered.

Flag   A variable (usually Boolean) that is tested to determine whether a loop will be executed.

Infinite loop   A loop that will execute indefinitely. This occurs because the condition controlling loop execution never reaches the state necessary for the loop to stop executing.

Loop control variable (lcv)   A variable used to control the number of times a loop will be executed.

Priming read   A *read* statement used before entering an input loop to initialize the loop control variable.

Sentinel value   A special data value that is used to mark the end of input data.

REVIEW OF KEY TERMS

_____ occurs when a segment of a program is executed repeatedly. A(n)
(1)

_____ loop is executed a specified number of times whereas when a loop is
(2)

controlled by a(n) _____ value, it continues executing until this value is read.
(3)

A(n) _____ read is often executed before a loop is entered for the first time.
(4)

Another method of controlling loop repetition is by using a(n) _____ flag.
(5)

The value of this flag determines whether the loop will be executed. A(n)

_____ variable is used in counting loops to determine if the loop will be
(6)

executed. This variable is incremented (or decremented) each time the loop is executed. When

the condition controlling loop repetition never reaches the value needed to stop execution, a(n)

_____ loop occurs.
(7)

MULTIPLE CHOICE

1. The three types of loop statements are _____.
    a. *while/do*, *repeat/until*, and *for*
    b. *if/then/else*, *repeat/until*, and *for*
    c. *while/do*, *repeat/do*, and *for*
    d. *while/do*, *if/then*, and *for*

2. Which of the following is *not* true of the *while/do* loop?
    a. If its body is a compound statement, it must be enclosed in a *begin/end* pair.
    b. The condition controlling loop repetition is tested before the loop is entered.
    c. The body of the loop may not be a compound statement.
    d. It executes as long as the stated condition is true.

Use the following program segment to answer Questions 3-6. Assume that *Value* is of type *integer*.

```
Value := 14;
while Value >= 0 do
begin
   Value := Value - 3;
   write (Value:6)
end   (* while *)
```

3. How many statements are contained in the body of this loop?
    a. 1
    b. 2
    c. 4
    d. 5

4. How many times will this loop execute?
    a. zero times
    b. 6 times
    c. 5 times
    d. indefinitely

5. What will be output?
    a. 11 8 5 2 -1
    b. 14 11 8 5 2 -1
    c. 14 11 8 5 2
    d. 11 8 5 2

6. What would happen if the condition controlling loop repetition was changed to "while Value <= 0 do"?
    a. The loop would not execute at all.
    b. The loop would execute infinitely.
    c. The loop would execute 6 times.
    d. The loop would execute 5 times.

Use the following program segment to answer Questions 7-12.

```
for Value := 8 downto 3 do
begin
   Product := Value * 3;
   write (Product:5)
end   (* for *)
```

7. The loop control variable in this *for* loop is _____.
    a. 8
    b. 3
    c. Value
    d. There is no loop control variable.

8. The starting value is _____ and the terminal value is _____.
    a. 1, 8   c. 3, 8
    b. 8, 1   d. 8, 3

9. What will happen to the loop control variable each time this loop is executed?
    a. It will be incremented to the stopping point.
    b. It will be incremented by 3.
    c. It will be decremented to the next ordinal value.
    b. It will be incremented to the next ordinal value.

10. What is output by this program segment?
    a.   24   21   18   15   12   9   c.   8   7   6   5   4
    b.   9   12   15   18   21   24   d.   24   21   18   15   12

11. Which of the following *while/do* loops will obtain the same results as this *for* loop?

```
a.  Value := 8;                              c.  Value := 8;
    while Value <= 3 do                          while Value <= 3 do
    begin                                        begin
        Product := Value * 3;                        Product := Value * 3;
        write (Product:5);                           write (Product:5);
        Value := Value - 1                           Value := Value + 1
    end    (* while *)                           end    (* while *)



b.  Value := 8;                              d.  Value := 8;
    while Value > 3 do                           while Value >= 3 do
    begin                                        begin
        Product := Value * 3;                        Product := Value * 3;
        write (Product:5);                           write (Product:5);
        Value := Value - 1                           Value := Value - 1
    end    (* while *)                           end    (* while *)
```

12. Which of the following *repeat/until* loops will obtain the same results as this *for* loop?

```
a.  Value := 8;                              c.  Value := 8;
    repeat until Value < 3                       repeat
        Product := Value * 3;                        Product := Value * 3;
        write (Product:5);                           write (Product:5);
        Value := Value - 1                           Value := Value - 1
    end    (* repeat *)                      until Value <= 3



b.  Value := 8;                              d.  Value := 8;
    repeat                                       repeat
        Product := Value * 3;                    begin
        write (Product:5);                           Prodcut := Value * 3;
        Value := Value - 1                           write (Product:5);
    until Value < 3                               Value := Value - 1
                                             repeat until Value < 3
```

13. Which of the following is *not* true concerning *for* loops?
    a. The loop control variable can be any ordinal data type.
    b. The loop control variable must be of type *integer*.
    c. *For* loops can be nested inside of one another.
    d. When the *to* format is used, the loop control variable is incremented to the next ordinal value each time the loop is executed.

Use the following program segment to answer Questions 14 through 16. Assume that *Grade* is of type *char*.

```
readln (Grade);
repeat
    writeln ('Your grade is ', Grade);
    if Grade < 'C'
        then writeln ('Good grade.');
    readln (Grade)
until Grade = 'Z'
```

14. This program segment has a syntax error because _____.
    a. there must be a semicolon before the *until* clause
    b. there is no *begin* to indicate the start of the loop body
    c. the body of the loop may only be a single statement
    d. There is no syntax error.

15. This loop will continue executing until _____.
    a. *Grade* is greater than C
    b. the value Z is read to *Grade*
    c. the value C is read to *Grade*
    d. the value of *Grade* is less than C

16. This is an example of a(n) _____.
    a. counting loop
    b. loop controlled by a Boolean flag
    c. infinite loop
    d. loop controlled by a sentinel value

ASSIGNMENTS

Assignment 1

In 1987, the population of Mount Pleasant was 15,000. The rate of growth is 5% a year. Write a *while/do* loop that will calculate and print the population for each of the next ten years. Rewrite the program using a *repeat/until* and a *for* loop.

while/do loop

repeat/until loop

for loop

Assignment 2

Give the values of the variables **X** and **M** at the end of each loop repetition. Use the program segment below. (You may assume that **X** and **M** are of type *integer*.)

```
X := 40;
M := 2;
repeat
   X := X div M;
   X := X + 1;
   M := M + 2;
until M > X
```

Repetition #	Value of X (at the bottom of the loop)	Value of M (at the bottom of the loop)

DEBUGGING EXERCISES

Identify and correct the errors in the following programs or program segments.

1.
```
program SeasonStats (input, output);

var
    Game, Wins : integer;

begin    (* SeasonStats *)

    Game := 100;
    Wins := 0;
    while Game > 60 do
    begin
        Wins := Wins + 1;
        Game := Game + 5
    end;    (* while *)
    writeln ('Number of wins = ', Wins:5)

end.    (* SeasonStats *)
```

Use the following declarations for Exercises 2 and 3:

```
program Scores (input, output);

var
    IdNum, Class, Score, I : integer;
    AveScore, Totals, NumScore, X : real;
    Grade, Letter : char;
```

2.
```
begin    (* Scores *)

    for I := 1 to 15 do
        readln (IdNum, Score);
    writeln ('There were ', I:4, ' Scores.')

end.    (* Scores *)
```

3.
```
for I := 10 downto 1 do
    for I := 1 to 5 do
    begin
        read (Score);
        write (Score:4)
    end    (* for *)
```

PROGRAMMING PROBLEMS

1.   Write a program that will determine the first three perfect numbers. In order to be a perfect number, a positive integer must be equal to the sum of all the positive integers (excluding itself) which divide it evenly. The first perfect number is 6 (1 + 2 + 3 = 6).

2.   Write a procedure that determines if a positive integer is prime. The positive integer should be passed to the procedure and the procedure should then display a message stating whether the number is prime.

Chapter 7

Program Style, Testing and Numerical Accuracy

CHAPTER OBJECTIVES

After studying this chapter, you should be able to:

1. Write programs that use good programming style.
2. Explain what is meant by numerical accuracy.
3. Define representational error.
4. Explain how numerical underflow and overflow occur.
5. Define and identify the three types of program errors.
6. Determine boundary cases in control structures.
7. Describe the characteristics of a user-friendly program.
8. Write user-friendly programs.

KEY TERMS

Cancellation error   An error that occurs when working with real numbers that vary widely in size. The smaller number is sometimes cancelled out by the larger one.

Compile-time error   See **Syntax error**.

Crash   To stop executing prematurely.

External documentation   Documentation that explains the purpose of a program or how to use the program. It is not contained within the program itself and is often in paper form.

Internal documentation   Comments about a program that are contained within the program itself.

Logic error   A flaw in a program's algorithm.

Numerical overflow The condition when a number is too large for a computer to store in memory.

Numerical underflow The condition when a number is too small for a computer to store in memory.

Precision The number of digits in a number that are correct.

Program style A way of writing a program to make it easier for humans to understand. The style of a program does not affect the computer's ability to execute it.

Program tracing A method of locating program errors by using *writeln* statements.

Range All of the values between the largest and smallest values a computer system can represent.

Representational error An error caused by lack of precision in representing real numbers in the computer memory.

Run-time error An error that causes abnormal program behavior during execution.

Syntax error A violation of the grammatical rules of a language.

REVIEW OF KEY TERMS

Program _____ is concerned with the manner in which a program is
                    (1)

written to make it easier for people to understand. There are two types of documentation:

_____ documentation such as the comments contained in a program and
            (2)

_____ documentation such as user's manuals that explains how to use
            (3)

software. A(n) _____ error occurs when the programmer violates the
                    (4)

grammatical rules of a language whereas a(n) _____ error occurs when the
                                    (5)

program stops executing prematurely (or _____). When a program obtains
                            (6)

correct results sometimes and incorrect results others, it has a(n) _____ error.
                                            (7)

Inserting *writeln* statements in a program in an effort to locate errors is referred to as program

_____. When a program is easy to use and politely informs the user when an
            (8)

invalid value has been entered, it is _____. The precision of a number is the
                        (9)

maximum number of correct digits. When a computer system cannot accurately store a real

number because the number has too many decimal positions, a(n) _____ error
                                            (10)

has occurred. When a number is too large for the system to store, a numerical

_____ error occurs whereas when the number is too small, a numerical
            (11)

_____ error occurs. The numbers, from largest through smallest, that a
            (12)

system can represent is its _____.
                        (13)

MULTIPLE CHOICE

1. The purpose of using spacing and indentation in a program is to make the program _____.
   a. easier for the computer to execute
   b. execute faster
   c. easier for people to understand
   d. shorter

2. A user's manual for a Pascal compiler is an example of _____.
   a. external documentation
   b. good program style
   c. internal documentation
   d. using descriptive variable names

3. If the statement (* Read 25 addresses. *) were included in a Pascal program, it would be an example of _____.
   a. external documentation
   b. internal documentation
   c. using descriptive variable names
   d. a user-friendly program

4. Which of the following is *not* one of the three basic categories of program errors?
   a. syntax errors
   b. off-by-one errors
   c. run-time errors
   d. logic errors

5. The following program segment contains a(n) _____ error. (Assume **X** and **N** are of type *integer* and *Amount* is of type *real*.)

```
X := 5;
while X >= 9 do
begin
    readln (N);
    Amount := N / X;
    X := X - 1
end    (* while *)
```

   a. syntax
   b. run-time
   c. uninitialized variable
   d. typing

Use the following program segment to answer Questions 6 and 7.

```
program ChangeHeight (input, output);

const
    CentimetersPerInch = 2.54;

var
    HeightInCent, HeightInFeet : real;

begin  (* ChangeHeight *)

    write ('Enter your height in feet: ');
    readln (HeightInFeet);
    HeightInCent := HeightInFeet * CentimetersPerInch;
    writeln ('Your height in centimeters is ', HeightInCent:6:2)
```

6. This program segment contains a _____ error.
   a. division by zero
   b. run-time
   c. logic
   d. syntax

7. This program segment could be correct by _____.
   a. multiplying *HeightInFeet* by 12 before performing the conversion
   b. making *CentimetersPerInch* a variable rather than a constant
   c. dividing *HeightInFeet* by *CentimetersPerInch* instead of multiplying it by *CentimetersPerInch*
   d. reading the value entered by the user to *HeightInCent* rather than *HeightInFeet*

8. What is wrong with the following program?

```
program Backwards (input, output);

var
  X : Integer;

begin  (* Backwards *)

   while X >= 0 do
   begin
      X := X - 4;
      write (X:5)
   end    (* while *)

   end.    (* Backwards *)
```

   a. The variable **X** must be incremented during each loop repetition instead of decremented.
   b. The variable **X** must be of type *real*.
   c. **X** is not initialized before the loop is entered.
   d. There is nothing wrong with this program.

9. Which of the following is *not* one of the three cases that should be checked for when using selective program testing?
   a. the illegal case
   b. the null case
   c. run-time cases
   d. boundary cases

10. Checking for illegal cases basically means determining if _____.
    a. the user has entered data within the range that the program can use
    b. a run-time error has occurred
    c. the program contains any syntax errors
    d. the program contains any logic errors

11. Precision refers to _____.
    a. the largest and smallest number a computer system can represent
    b. the number of significant digits in a number
    c. writing a real number in exponential notation
    d. the situation in which a number is too large for the computer system to store

12. When a number is too large for the computer system to store _____ has occurred.
    a. numerical underflow
    b. a representational error
    c. numerical overflow
    d. a logic error

ASSIGNMENTS

Assignment 1

Make the following program more understandable by inserting spacing and indentation where appropriate.

```
program CarWash (input, output);

const
Wash=2.50;
Wax=2.00;
Vacuum=1.50;
Windows=1.50;
Senior= 0.15;
var
Cost:real;
Answer,More:char;
begin
repeat
Cost:=0.0;
write('Is this car to be washed? Y/N: ');
readln(Answer);
if Answer='Y'
then Cost:=Cost+Wash;
write('Is this car to be waxed? Y/N: ');
readln(Answer);
if Answer='Y'
then Cost:=Cost+Wax;
write('Is car to be vacuumed inside? Y/N: ');
readln(Answer);
if Answer='Y'
then Cost:=Cost+Vacuum;
write('Are inside windows to be washed? Y/N: ');
readln(Answer);
if Answer='Y'
then Cost:=Cost+Windows;
write('Is this person a senior citizen? Y/N: ');
readln(Answer);
if Answer='Y'
then Cost:=Cost-Cost*Senior;
writeln('The total bill for cleaning this car is ',Cost:7:2);
write('Are there more bills to calculate? Y/N: ');
readln(More)
until More='N'
end.
```

Assignment 2

Every computer system has a maximum size for integer values. This value is assigned the name *MaxInt*. Determine what this value is on your system. You can do this by executing the statement: writeln (MaxInt). Also consult your system documentation to determine the range of real numbers that your computer is capable of storing. Then fill in the table below.

	Integers	Real Numbers
Smallest		
Largest		

DEBUGGING EXERCISES

Find one run-time and one logic error in the following program.

```
program Race (Input, output);

var
    Diff, LapTime, Rec, RecTime, Total : real;
    Laps, I : Integer;

begin   (* Race *)

    write ('Number of laps In race: ');
    readln (Laps);
    write ('Record time In race: ');
    readln (Rec);
    RecTime := Rec / Laps;
    for I := 1 to Laps do
    begin
       write ('Time for lap ', I, ': ');
       readln (LapTime);
       Total := Total + LapTime;
       Diff := LapTime - RecTime;
       If Diff < 0
           then writeln (Diff:8:2, ' seconds off record lap time.')
           else writeln (Diff:8:2, ' seconds faster than record lap time.')
    end;   (* for *)
    writeln ('Time: ', Total:8:2);
    If Total < Rec
        then writeln ('NEW RECORD!')

end.   (* Race *)
```

PROGRAMMING PROBLEMS

1.   A public library would like a program that calculates the total cost of books it adds to its collection. This includes not only the basic price of the book, but also the cost of processing the book. Processing costs are dependent on two factors:

   1. The type of book (reference, circulating, or paperback);
   2. Whether or not the book is a duplicate of one already in the library.

It is cheaper to process books that are duplicates of ones already in the collection because cards for these books are already in the card catalog. Therefore, the cost of producing new cards is saved. Processing costs are as follows:

Reference book
    not a duplicate $8.50
    duplicate $7.40

Circulating book
    not a duplicate $7.82
    duplicate $6.60
    bestseller $1.75   additional

Paperback
    not a duplicate $4.60
    duplicate $3.10

The type of book will be entered using a code number:

1 - Reference
2 - Circulating
3 - Paperback

Note the additional $1.75 cost for processing circulating books that are bestsellers. This is for a plastic cover for added protection. The program should round the processing cost to the nearest tenth of a dollar to make bookkeeping simpler. The total cost should be displayed on the screen.

2.   Write a program that can be used by a fast-food restaurant to calculate customer bills. The program should display a menu similar to the following:

   1. Hamburgers   80 cents
   2. Cheeseburgers   95 cents
   3. French fries   75 cents
   4. Small drink   70 cents
   5. Large drink   90 cents
   6. Order completed.

The user should be prompted to enter the integer value representing the desired item. The program should then prompt the user to enter the quantity of that item needed. The menu should be displayed again so that the user can make another choice. When the number 6 is entered, the total cost should be displayed, including a 6% sales tax.

Chapter 8

More on Modularization

CHAPTER OBJECTIVES

After studying this chapter, you should be able to:

1.   Use the standard functions introduced in this chapter.
2.   Explain how the *pred*, *succ*, *ord*, and *chr* functions work.
3.   Write user-defined functions.
4.   Trace a nested block structure.
5.   Identify the scope of any variable declared in a program.
6.   Define the terms local variable and global variable.
7.   Use stubs in developing programs.
8.   Give a definition of enumerated data types.
9.   Appropriately use enumerated data types in programs.
10. Discuss the limitations of using enumerated data types.
11. Give a definition of subrange data types.
12. Appropriately use subrange data types in programs.

KEY TERMS

Call by location   The process of passing a variable parameter, in which the address of the variable in the calling program is passed to the subprogram rather than the value itself.

Call by reference   See **Call by location**.

Call by value   The process of passing a value parameter, in which only the value is passed to the subprogram, where a new storage location is set up for the value. After the subprogram is finished executing, the contents of the storage location are discarded.

Driver program   A program whose primary purpose is to reference subprograms.

Enumerated data type   An ordinal data type that is defined by the programmer to meet a particular need. Every possible value of the data type must be listed in the definition.

Function   A subprogram used to return a single value to the calling program.

Function call   An expression that causes a function to be executed.

Scope block   The portion of a program in which a particular identifier is defined.

Side effect   An unintended change to a nonlocal variable in a subprogram.

Stub   A procedure or function declaration that contains only a header, a *begin-end* pair, and possibly a *writeln* statement which says that the procedure was called. It is used to test the calling routine.

Subrange data type   A data type defined by the programmer that contains a portion of an ordinal data type.

User-defined data type   See **Enumerated data type**.

REVIEW OF KEY TERMS

A subprogram that returns a single value is a(n) _____ and is executed by
(1)

using a(n) _____ . The situation in which a parameter does not return its value
(2)

to the calling program is _____ ; when the value is returned to the calling
(3)

program, _____ has occurred. The portion of a program in which a particular
(4)

identifier is defined is its _____ block. When a nonlocal variable is altered in
(5)

a subprogram a(n) _____ has occurred. A common method of developing a
(6)

large program is to add the subprograms a few at a time. It can then be determined whether the

subprograms are working properly before more are added. Before a subprogram is inserted in a

program it is represented by a(n) _____ which usually contains the
(7)

subprogram's heading and a *writeln* statement indicating that it was called. A program whose

main purpose is to call subprograms is a(n) _____ program.
(8)

_____ data types are defined by the programmer; every possible value for that
(9)

type must be listed in the definition. _____ data types contain a portion of a
(10)

predefined or enumerated data type.

MULTIPLE CHOICE

1. What is wrong with the following function heading?
   function Total (Ave1, Ave2, Percent : real);
   a. The variable *Total* is a reserved identifier.
   b. The parameters *Ave1*, *Ave2*, and *Percent* must be *var* parameters.
   c. The function does not have a type.
   d. There is nothing wrong with this function heading.

2. Which of the following is *not* true of functions?
   a. They can be of any standard data type.
   b. They can have any number of parameters.
   c. They return a single value to the calling program.
   d. They must be of type *real*.

3. *Round* is an example of a(n) _____.
   a. standard function
   b. Boolean function
   c. arithmetic operator
   d. user-defined function

Use the following program segment to answer Questions 4-8.

```
program Example (input, output);

var
    Side : real;
    I1, I2 : integer;
    N1, N2 : real;
    B1 : boolean;

function SurfaceArea (Side : real) : real;
(* Calculates the surface area of a cube . *)

begin   (* SurfaceArea *)

    SurfaceArea := (Side * Side) * 6

end;   (* SurfaceArea *)

begin   (* Example *)

    write ('Enter the length of the cube''s side: ');
    readln (Side);
    writeln (SurfaceArea (Side):6:2);

    N1 := 98.80;
    I1 := trunc (N1);
    B1 := odd (I1);
    N2 := abs (N1);
    I2 := pred (I1)
```

4. *SurfaceArea* is an example of a(n) _____ function.
   a. standard
   b. user-defined
   c. invalid
   d. built-in

5. If the value of *Side* is 4, what value will *SurfaceArea* return to the calling program?
    a. 48
    b. 96
    c. 24
    d. No value will be returned to the calling program.

6. What will the value of *I1* be after this program segment is executed?
    a. -98
    b. 99
    c. 98
    d. even

7. What will the value of *B1* be after this program segment is executed?
    a. true
    b. false
    c. 98
    d. 99

8. What will the value of *N2* be after this program segment is executed?
    a. 98.80
    b. -98.80
    c. 98
    d. true

9. What will the value of *I2* be after this program segment is executed?
    a. 98
    b. true
    c. 99
    d. 97

10. Which of the following standard functions never returns a real value?
    a. sqrt
    b. exp
    c. odd
    d. abs

11. The function *pred* can be used with variables of _____.
    a. any standard data type
    b. any ordinal data type
    c. type *integer* only
    d. type *real* only

12. The value returned by the *chr* function _____.
    a. depends on the collating sequence of the computer system
    b. is always of type *boolean*
    c. depends on the data type of the argument
    d. is always of type *real*

13. The scope block of an identifier determines _____.
    a. its data type
    b. its value
    c. the portion of the program in which it is defined
    d. whether it is a value or variable parameter

Use the following declarations to answer Questions 14-16.

```
type
    AnimalType = (Horse, Mouse, Dog, Pig, Sparrow, Finch, Robin);
    MammalType = Horse .. Pig;
    BirdType = Sparrow .. Robin;

var
    Animals : AnimalType;
    Mammals : MammalType;
    Birds   : BirdType;
```

14. *AnimalType* is a(n) _____ data type and *MammalType* is a(n) _____ data type.
    a. subrange, enumerated
    b. enumerated, subrange
    c. enumerated, integer
    d. char, enumerated

15. How many different values is it possible for the variable *Bird* to have?
    a. 3
    b. 7
    c. 4
    d. an infinite number

16. If the value of *Animals* is Horse, what will be output by the following statement?
        writeln (ord(Animals))
    a. 1
    b. Horse
    c. 0
    d. Mouse

ASSIGNMENTS

Assignment 1

Draw boxes around the scope blocks
in the following program. Then fill in the
table indicating which constants, variables,
functions, and procedures are defined in
which scope blocks.

```
program Main (input, output);
const
   C1 = 475;
   C2 = 14.5;

var
   V1, V2 : real;
   V3, V4 : char;


procedure P1;

var
   V5, V6 : integer;
   V7 : real;


function F1 : real;

var
   V8 : real;

begin   (* F1 *)
 .
 .
 .
end;    (* F1 *)


begin    (* P1 *)
 .
 .
end;   (* P1 *)
const
   C3 = 'F';

var
   V8, V9 : char;
   V10    : real;

procedure P3;

procedure P4;

var
   V11 : integer;
   V12 : char;

begin   (* P4 *)
 .
 .
 .
end;   (* P4 *)


begin   (* P3 *)
 .
 .
 .
end;   (* P3 *)


begin   (* P2 *)
 .
 .
end;   (* P2 *)


begin   (* Main *)
 .
 .
 .
end.   (* Main *)
```

Assignment 1 (cont.)

Subprogram Name	Variables and Constants Defined in this Subprogram	Variables and Constants Local to this Subprogram
Main		
P1		
P2		
P3		
P4		
F1		

Assignment 2

Evaluate the results of the function calls listed in the table. Use the declarations below.

```
type
    ClassType = (Freshman, Sophomore, Junior, Senior);

var
    I1, I2 : Integer;
    R1, R2 : real;
    C1 : char;
    Class : ClassType;
```

Function Call	**Value Returned**
1. pred(succ('M'))	
2. sqrt (3 * 3 * 9)	
3. abs (180.5 - 92.25)	
4. trunc (180.5 - 92.25)	
5. ord (Sophomore)	
6. round (7 * 1.75)	
7. sqr (4.5)	
8. pred (Junior)	
9. odd (19 - 3)	
10. succ (trunc (-198.6))	

DEBUGGING EXERCISES

Identify and correct the errors in the following programs.

1.
```
program Root (input, output);

var
    Number, Sqroot : integer;

function FindRoot (Num : integer) : real;

begin   (* FindRoot *)

   FindRoot := sqrt (Num)

end;   (* FindRoot *)

begin   (* main *)

   readln (Number);
   if Number > 0
      then Sqroot := FindRoot (Number)
      else writeln ('No real root for ', Number:5)

end.   (* main *)
```

2.
```
program Dimensions (input, output);

var
    Cutoff, Side, CubeVolume : real;
    Area, Num : integer;

begin   (* Dimensions *)

    readln (Num);
    Num := odd (Num);
    if Num
       then writeln (Num, ' is odd.')
       else writeln (Num, ' is even.')

end.   (* Dimensions *)
```

PROGRAMMING PROBLEMS

1.   The constant pi can be approximated by the following formula:

$$\frac{\pi^2}{6} = 1 + \frac{1}{2^2} + \frac{1}{3^2} + \frac{1}{4^2} + \frac{1}{5^2} \ldots$$

Write a procedure that will perform this calculation for 200 values and print the resulting value of pi.

2.   Write a program that calls a function to determine the distance a car has traveled. Assume that the car starts at rest. The user should be prompted to enter the acceleration and amount of time lapsed. A function should be called to calculate the distance based on the formula:

distance = 1/2 acceleration x time^2

A second function should then be called to calculate the velocity:

velocity = acceleration x time

The main program should then display both of these values with appropriate labels.

Chapter 9

Arrays

CHAPTER OBJECTIVES

After studying this chapter, you should be able to:

1. Explain the difference between a simple data type and a structured data type.
2. Define and use one-dimensional arrays.
3. Read data to the elements of an array.
4. Output the values stored in array elements.
5. Correctly evaluate and use array subscripts.
6. Define and use multidimensional arrays.
7. Use the bubble sort to place the contents of an array in ascending or descending order.
8. Search an array for a specified value.

KEY TERMS

Array An ordered collection of related values, having a common variable name, all of the same data type.

Bubble sort A type of sort in which adjacent array elements are compared. If the elements are out of order, they are switched. This process is repeated until the entire array is in order.

Element An individual value in an array.

Index See **Subscript**.

Linear search See **Sequential search**.

Packed array An array in which two or more elements are stored in each storage location.

Primitive data type See **Simple data type**.

Scalar data type   Any standard or user-defined data type having values that can be placed in order, although a given value need not have a unique predecessor or successor.

Sequential search   Searching through a list beginning with the first element and comparing each consecutive element with the target value until a match is found.

Simple data type   Any standard or user-defined data type that can contain only a single element, such as a real number or a single character.

Structured data type   A data type that can be broken into smaller components. The structured data types in Pascal are arrays, records, sets, and files.

Subscript   A value placed in brackets after the name of an array; it is used to reference a particular array element.

REVIEW OF KEY TERMS

When the values in a particular data type can be placed in order, the data type is

_____. _____ data types are composed of smaller
        (1)   (2)

components. Data types that cannot be broken into smaller components are

_____ data types. A(n) _____ is an ordered collection of
      (3)   (4)

related values of the same type; its individual values are _____. To reference
            (5)

these individual values a(n) _____ is used. Character strings are often stored
          (6)

in _____ arrays that can be directly compared to one another. Arranging
     (7)

values in a particular order is _____ them. The _____
            (8)   (9)

orders the elements in an array by repeatedly comparing adjacent elements and exchanging them

if they are out of order. _____ an array involves attempting to locate a
         (10)

specified value in it. In a(n) _____, each array element from first to last is
        (11)

compared to the target value until the target is found.

MULTIPLE CHOICE

1. The individual values in an array are called the array _____.
   a. subscripts
   b. variables
   c. positions
   d. elements

2. Which of the following is *not* true of an array?
   a. It allows for a group of related values to be referred to by a single variable name.
   b. It is a structured data type.
   c. The elements cannot be of type *real*.
   d. The array elements are stored in adjacent memory locations.

3. What characteristic do all simple data types share?
   a. They are all ordinal data types.
   b. They cannot be broken into smaller components.
   c. Their values are always numeric (*real* or *integer*).
   d. They are composed of individual elements all of the same data type.

Use the following program segment to answer Questions 4-7.

```
type
    Sub = 'm' .. 'q';
    ArrayType = array[Sub] of Integer;

var
    Values : ArrayType;
```

4. Array *Values* is of type _____.
   a. integer
   b. char
   c. ArrayType
   d. Sub

5. The elements of array *Values* are of type _____.
   a. integer
   b. char
   c. ArrayType
   d. Sub

6. The subscripts of *Values* are of type _____.
   a. integer
   b. char
   c. ArrayType
   d. Sub

7. What is the maximum number of elements that can be stored in *Values*?
   a. 4
   b. 5
   c. It depends on the number of integers that the computer can represent.
   d. 6

8. Which of the following statements will assign the value 118 to the third element of array *Values*?
   a. Values[succ('n')] := 118
   b. ArrayType['o'] := 118
   c. Values[pred('n')] := 118
   d. Values[o] := 118

9. Which of the following program segments could be used to search the array *Values* for the element containing 54 and store its subscript in a variable named *Position*. (Assume *Current* and *Position* are both of type *Sub*.)

```
a. for Current := 'm' to 'q' do
      if Values[Position] = 54
         then Position := Current
```

```
c. for Position := 'm' to 'q' do
      if Values[Current] = 54
         then Position := Current
```

```
b. for Current := 'm' to 'q' do
      if Values[Current] = 54
         then Current := Position
```

```
d. for Current := 'm' to 'q' do
      if Values[Current] = 54
         then Position := Current
```

10. The type of search used in Question 9 is a(n) _____ search.
    a. simple
    b. sequential
    c. bubble
    d. integer

11. In a two-dimensional array, the first subscript indicates the _____ and the second subscript indicates the _____.
    a. row, column
    b. column, row
    c. element, row
    d. column, element

Use the following program segment to answer Question 12.

```
var
    Customers : array[1..6,9..17] of Integer;
    Day, Hours : Integer;

begin
    for Day := 1 to 6 do
       for Hours := 9 to 17 do
          readln (Customers[Day, Hours])
```

12. What is the maximum number of elements that array Customers can have?
    a. 6
    b. 48
    c. 54
    d. 14

ASSIGNMENTS

Assignment 1

Use the following program segment to fill in the table on page 149.

```
program SaveTemp (input, output);

type
    DayType = (Sunday, Monday, Tuesday, Wednesday, Thursday, Friday,
               Saturday);
    HourRange = 1..24;
    ArrayType = array[DayType,HourRange] of real;

var
    Day : DayType;
    Hour : HourRange;
    Temperature : ArrayType;

begin

    Temperature[Monday, 16+4] := 70.2;

    Temperature[pred (Friday), ord (Saturday)] := 75.4;

    Temperature[Tuesday, pred (22+2)] := 69.5;

    Temperature[succ (Monday), 8*2] := 71.2;

    Temperature[Thursday, succ (ord (Sunday))] := 70;

    Temperature[succ (succ (Wednesday)), 30-20] := 72.3
```

Assignment 1 (cont.)

Day	Hour 1	2	3	4	5	6	7	8	9	10	11	12	13	14	15	16	17	18	19	20	21	22	23	24
Sun.																								
Mon.																								
Tues.																								
Wed.																								
Thur.																								
Fri.																								
Sat.																								

Assignment 2

The statements in the following bubble sort have been scrambled. See if you can unscramble them. This bubble sort is supposed to sort an array of character strings (Companies) in alphabetical order.

```
program Sort (Input, output);

const
    MaxNum = 20;

type
    Str30 = packed array[1..30] of char;

var
    Companies : array[1..MaxNum] of Str30;
    Exchange : boolean;
    Num, NumPass, Position : integer;
    Temp : Str30;

begin

    NumPass := Num - 1;
    repeat

        for Position := 1 to MaxNum do
        begin
            Exchange := false;
            if Companies[Position] > Companies[Position+1]
                then
                begin
                    Companies[Position+1] := Temp;
                    Temp := Companies[Position];
                    Companies[Position] := Companies[Position+1]
                end;    (* then *)
            Exchange := true
        end    (* for *)

    until Exchange = false;
    NumPass := NumPass - 1

end.    (* Sort *)
```

DEBUGGING EXERCISES

Identify and correct the errors in the following program segment. Use the following program segment for Exercises 1 and 2.

```
program Cities (input, output);

type
    City = array[1..10] of integer;

var
    Pop : City;
    Count, I : integer;
```

1. ```
   begin   (* Cities *)

       Count := 0;
           while Count <= 10 do
           begin
               read (Pop[Count]);
               Count := Count + 1
           end   (* while *)
   ```

2. ```
   begin   (* Cities *)

       City[1] := 2489;
       City[8] := 29462;
       City[4] := 869
   ```

PROGRAMMING PROBLEMS

1.   Write a program that reads a list of test scores. The following should then be determined and displayed:

   a. The mean (average) of all scores
   b. The mode (most commonly occurring score)
   c. The range (the smallest and largest score)

2.   The Tri-State Gymnastics Competition needs a program to calculate the average scores of competitors in its meets. Each competitor is awarded a score (out of a possible 10 points) by each of six judges. The average score is determined by discarding the highest and lowest scores and calculating the average of the other four. Allow the user to enter the competitor's number and each judge's score at the keyboard. The output should be similar to this:

Competitor number 48 has an average score of 8.95.

Chapter 10

Files

CHAPTER OBJECTIVES

After studying this chapter, you should be able to:

1. Define a file.
2. Discuss the advantages and disadvantages of using files.
3. Explain how a file buffer variable is used to access file components.
4. Create text files and read and write data to them.
5. Explain the differences between binary and text files.
6. Create binary files and read and write data to them.

KEY TERMS

File   A sequence of components, all of the same data type, stored in auxiliary storage.

File buffer variable   A variable that can be thought of as a "window" to a file. It allows a single file component to be accessed.

REVIEW OF KEY TERMS

_____ have a distinct advantage over arrays because they are kept in
(1)

auxiliary storage. When a file is created, a(n) _____ variable is also created
(2)

through which a single file component can be accessed.

MULTIPLE CHOICE

1. Which of the following is *not* a characteristic of a file?
   a. Files are generally kept in secondary storage.
   b. Files in secondary storage take longer to access than arrays in main memory.
   c. Files allow large quantities of data to be stored relatively inexpensively.
   d. Files are easier and faster to access than arrays.

2. On interactive systems, the standard file _____ reads data entered at the keyboard and _____ displays results on the monitor screen.
   a. input, output
   b. output, input
   c. text, output
   d. input, text

3. The components of the standard file type *text* are of type _____.
   a. integer
   b. real
   c. char
   d. string

4. Which of the following is *not* true of sequential files?
   a. New file components can be inserted anywhere in the file.
   b. Data is stored in the file in the order in which it is read.
   c. In order to access the twentieth component of a sequential file, the nineteen components in front of it must be accessed first.
   d. New file components may only be added to the end of the file.

5. A file buffer variable _____.
   a. determines how many components are contained in a file
   b. is always of type *integer*
   c. is like a window that allows a single file component to be accessed
   d. closes and permanently saves the contents of a file

6. The *eof* and *eoln* functions are both _____ functions.
   a. integer
   b. Boolean
   c. user-defined
   d. character

Use the following program to answer Questions 7-10.

```
program ReadFile (Poetry, output);

var
    Poetry : text;
    Next : char;

begin   (* ReadFile *)

    reset (Poetry);
    while not eof (Poetry) do
    begin
        while not eoln (Poetry) do
        begin
            read (Poetry, Next);
            write (Next)
        end;   (* inner while *)
        readln (Poetry);
        writeln
    end    (* outer while *)

end.  (* ReadFile *)
```

7. The file *Poetry* is a(n) _____.
   a. internal file
   b. file of integers
   c. variable file
   d. external file

8. What is the function of the statement "reset (Poetry)"?
   a. It saves the file *Poetry* on disk.
   b. It prepares the file *Poetry* to be written to.
   c. It prepares the file *Poetry* to be read from.
   d. It makes the file *Poetry* an external file.

9. If an interactive system is used, program *ReadFile* reads data from the _____ and writes output to the _____.
   a. keyboard, file *Poetry*
   b. file *Poetry*, monitor screen
   c. file *text*, file *Poetry*
   d. file *text*, monitor screen

10. The statement "read (Poetry, Next)" could be replaced with which of the following?
    a. Next := Poetry^;
       get (Poetry)
    b. Next := Poetry;
       get (Poetry)
    c. Poetry^ := Next;
       put (Poetry)
    d. get (Poetry);
       Next := Poetry^

11. The components of binary files are stored as _____.
    a. the binary equivalent of their values
    b. the ASCII equivalent of their values
    c. characters
    d. arrays

12. Which of the following is a major disadvantage of using binary files?
    a. Unlike text files, they cannot be created by typing data directly in at the keyboard.
    b. They take longer for the computer to access than text files.
    c. They can only contain numeric data.
    d. They can only contain character data.

Use the following program segment to answer Questions 13-15.

```
program StoreNumbers (Input, IFile);

type
    IntegerFile = file of Integer;

var
    IFile : IntegerFile;
    Number : real;
    I : Integer;

begin   (* StoreNumbers *)

    rewrite (IFile);
    write ('Enter a number: ');
    readln (Number);
    while Number <> -2000 do
    begin
        I := round (Number);
        IFile^ := I;
        put (IFile);
        write ('Enter the next number: ');
        readln (Number)
    end    (* while *)

end.    (* StoreNumbers *)
```

13. The components of file *IFile* are _____.
    a. characters
    b. strings
    c. integer
    d. real numbers

14. Which of the following best explains what this program does?
    a. It reads a file of real numbers, rounds them and outputs the results on the monitor screen.
    b. It reads a series of real numbers entered at the keyboard, rounds them, and writes the results to file *IFile*.
    c. It reads a file of integers and displays them on the monitor screen.
    d. It reads a series of integers entered at the keyboard, truncates them, and writes the results to file *IFile*.

ASSIGNMENTS

Assignment 1

Explain the purpose of each of the statements in the following table.

Statement	Purpose

var
    Phrases : text;
    Letter : char;	

reset (Phrases);	
while not eof (Phrases) do	
while not eoln (Phrases) do	
read (Phrases, Letter)	
readln (Phrases)	

Assignment 2

Declare files of the following types:

Descriptions	Declarations
1. A file containing the final scores of soccer matches (integer values).	
2. A file containing the names of plants (the names will have no more than 20 characters).	
3. A file whose components are Boolean arrays, each representing a binary digit (0 = false, 1 = true).	
4. A file whose components are of the enumerated type *Color* which is defined below: type Color = (Brown, Yellow, Orange, Purple, Pink, Lavender);	

DEBUGGING EXERCISES

Identify and correct the errors in the following programs and program segments.

1.
```
program AbsValue (NumIn, output);

var
    NumIn : file of integer;
    N : integer;

begin

    while not eof (NumIn) do
    begin
        reset (NumIn);
        N := NumIn^;
        get (NumIn);
        write (abs(N):7)
    end    (* while *)
```

2.
```
program AddUp (NumIn, output);

var
    NumIn : text;
    Amount, Tot : real;

begin    (* AddUp *)

    reset (NumIn);
    while not eof (NumIn) do
    begin
        while not eoln do
        begin
            read (NumIn, Amount);
            Tot := Tot + Amount
        end;    (* inner while *)
        readln (NumIn)
    end;    (* outer while *)

    writeln ('The total is: ', Tot:8:2)

end.    (* AddUp *)
```

PROGRAMMING PROBLEMS

1.   Write a program that saves the runs, hits, and errors for each inning of a nine-inning baseball game in a file named Games. The program should summarize the results of the game in a table that is displayed on the screen. The table should be labeled similar to the following:

	Runs		Hits		Errors	
	Home	Visitor	Home	Visitor	Home	Visitor

Innings

```
1
2
3
4
5
6
7
8
9
```

2.   Write a program that will read a list of numbers from a file and store them in two 5 x 4 matrices. The program should then give the user the choice of the following:

   1.   Adding the matrices
   2.   Subtracting the second matrix from the first one

If you are not certain how these matrix operations are performed, ask your mathematics teacher or refer to a matrix algebra book.

Chapter 11

Records, Sets, and Graphics

CHAPTER OBJECTIVES

After studying this chapter, you should be able to:

1. Declare and use records in programs.
2. Reference the individual fields of a record.
3. Use variant records.
4. Use sets in programs when appropriate.
5. Be able to use the set operators, +, *, and -.
6. Be able to use the set relational operators =, >=, <=, and < >.
7. Explain what is meant by graphics mode.
8. Discuss some features that are generally available in graphics packages.

KEY TERMS

Base type An ordinal data type used in declaring a set data type. It specifies the list of values or range of values that can be used with that set type.

Field A single data item that is a part of a record.

Field selector A record variable name and a field name, separated by a period. Used to identify a specific field within a record.

Pixel The smallest division of the screen in graphics mode that can be turned off or on.

Record A structured data type that allows a group of related data items, not necessarily of the same data type, to be referenced by a single name.

Set A collection of items, all of the same base type.

Subset   Set A is a subset of set B if every element of set A is also an element of set B.

Superset   Set A is a superset of set B if every element of set B is also an element of set A.

REVIEW OF KEY TERMS

A(n) _____ allows a group of related data of different types to be
        (1)

referenced as a single unit. The individual items stored in a record are its

_____ and can be referenced by using a(n) _____. A(n)
        (2)   (3)

_____ is a collection of like-type objects; each set's _____
        (4)   (5)

type consists of the values that can belong to that set. A set is a(n) _____ of
                                                                              (6)

another set if all of the values in the first set are contained in the second set. If a set contains all

of the values in a second set, it is a(n) _____ of the second set.
                                              (7)

_____ can be used to display illustrations, charts, and so forth on a monitor
        (8)

screen. The illustrations are created by turning on and off tiny _____ or
                                                                        (9)

rectangular blocks that make up the screen.

MULTIPLE CHOICE

1. An advantage that records have over arrays is _____ .
   a. not all of the fields of a record need be of the same data type
   b. they are faster for the computer to access
   c. they are easier for the programmer to use
   d. they are not limited in size

Use the following declarations to answer Questions 2-6.

```
type
     Str = packed array[1..20] of char;
     CityRec = record;
         City : Str;
         Pop : Integer;
         State : Str
     end;    (* CityRec *)

     CityArray = array[1..100] of CityRec;

var
     CityInfo : CityArray;
     Count : Integer;
```

2. What is the syntax error in the definition of the record type *CityRec*?
   a. There should be a *begin* after the first line.
   b. There should not be an *end* at the end of the record definition.
   c. The statement "CityRec = record" should be "CityRec : record"
   d. There should not be a semicolon after the reserved identifier *record*.

3. *CityInfo* is a(n) _____ .
   a. record of type *CityRec*
   b. array of records of type *CityRec*
   c. record of type *CityArray*
   d. array of records of type *Str*

4. The record type *CityRec* has _____ fields.
   a. 100
   b. 2
   c. 20
   d. 3

5. Which of the following statements will assign the value 2350 to the *Pop* field of the fourth record in array *CityInfo*?
   a. CityInfo[4].Pop := 2350
   b. CityInfo[4].CityRec.Pop := 2350
   c. CityInfo.Pop[4] := 2350
   d. CityInfo.CityRec.Pop[4] := 2350

6. Which of the following program segments will allow the user to enter the name of a city at the keyboard? The name should then be stored in the *City* field of the first record in the array *CityInfo*. (Assume that *Count* is of type *integer*.)

a.
```
Count := 1;
write ('Enter city''s name: ');
while not eoln do
begin
     read (CityInfo[1].City[Count]);
     Count := Count + 1
end;    (* while *)
readln
```

c.
```
Count := 1;
write ('Enter city''s name: ');
while not eoln do
begin
     read (City[Count]);
     Count := Count + 1
end;    (* while *)
readln
```

b.
```
Count := 1;
write ('Enter city''s name: ');
while not eoln do
begin
     read (CityInfo[1]);
     Count := Count + 1
end;    (* while *)
readln
```

d.
```
Count := 1;
write ('Enter city''s name: ');
while not eoln do
begin
     read (CityInfo[Count].City);
     Count := Count + 1
end;    (* while *)
readln
```

7. When copying one record to another, which of the following is true?
   a. Each field in the first record must be assigned to the corresponding field in the second record.
   b. A single assignment statement can be used to copy the entire contents of the first record to the second record.
   c. It is not possible to copy one record to another.
   d. Each character in the first record must be assigned to the corresponding position in the second record.

8. _____ records allow specified fields to vary depending on the needs of the situation.
   a. Fixed
   b. Variable
   c. Variant
   d. Packed

9. Which of the following is not a set operator?
   a. < >
   b. >=
   c. in
   d. /

Use the following program segment to answer Questions 10-14.

```
type
    IRange = 1..30;
    IValues = set of IRange;

var
    Primes : IValues;
    SmPrimes : IValues;
    LgPrimes : IValues;

begin
    Primes := [1, 3, 5, 7, 11, 13, 17, 19, 23];
    SmPrimes := [1, 3, 5, 7, 11, 13, 17];
    LgPrimes := [13, 17, 19, 23]
```

10. _____ is a subset of _____.
   a. SmPrimes, LgPrimes
   b. LgPrimes, SmPrimes
   c. SmPrimes, Primes
   d. Primes, SmPrimes

11. The expression "SmPrimes * LgPrimes" evaluates as _____.
    a. [13,17]
    b. [1, 3, 5, 7, 11, 13, 17, 19, 23]
    c. [ ]
    d. [1, 3, 5, 7, 11, 19, 23]

12. The expression "SmPrimes + LgPrimes" evaluates as _____.
    a. [13,17]
    b. [1, 3, 5, 7, 11, 13, 17, 19, 23]
    c. [ ]
    d. [1, 3, 5, 7, 11, 19, 23]

13. The expression Primes - SmPrimes evaluates as _____.
    a. [1, 3, 5, 7, 11, 13, 17]
    b. [19, 23]
    c. [ ]
    d. [1, 3, 5, 7, 11, 19, 23]

14. The expression "if 17 in SmPrimes" evaluates as _____.
    a. [1, 3, 5, 7, 11, 13]
    b. [ ]
    c. true
    d. false

15. Which of the following is generally not an appropriate use of graphics?
    a. creating illustrations
    b. performing text processing
    c. creating charts to visually illustrate program results
    d. graphing a function

ASSIGNMENTS

Assignment 1

A baseball team needs a file of records to store their team's statistics. The problem is that different statistics are needed for the batters than are needed for the pitchers. The following two fields are used for all the records:

Player's name
Player's number

The fields needed for the batters are:

Times at bats
Numbers of hits
Number of bases
Number of walks
Slugging percentage (Number of bases / Times at bat)
Batting average (Number of hits / Times at bat)

The fields needed for the pitchers are:

Innings pitched
Runs allowed
Number of strikeouts
Earned run average ((Innings pitched / Runs allowed) / 9)
Strikeout ratio ((Innings pitched / Number of strikeouts) * 9)

Define a variant record that can be used to store this data. Then declare a file of these records.

Assignment 2

Evaluate the expressions involving sets in the following table. Use the program segment below.

```
type
    SymbolSet = set of char;
var
    Symbols1, Symbols2 : SymbolSet;
begin
    Symbols1 := ['A', '*','M', '/', '&'];
    Symbols2 := ['*', '/', '&']
```

Expression	Evaluates as
1. Symbols1 >= ['A']	
2. 'L' in Symbols2	
3. Symbols1 >= Symbols2	
4. ['*', '/', '&'] < > Symbols2	
5. ['A', 'M'] - Symbols1	
6. Symbols1 + Symbols2	
7. Symbols2 * Symbols1	
8. Symbols1 * ['P', '-', ')']	

DEBUGGING EXERCISES

Identify and correct the errors in the following programs and program segments.

1.  ```pascal
    program TScore (Update, output);

    const
        MaxStu = 5;

    type
        StuRec = record
            StuNum : Integer;
            Test1 : real;
            Test2 : real;
            Total : real
        end;    (* record *)

        ClassRecs = array[1..MaxStu] of StuRec;

    var
        Class : ClassRecs;
        k : Integer;
    ```

2.  ```pascal
    program NumCnt (Input, output);

    type
        NumSet = set of 1..15;

    var
        Odd, Even : NumSet;

    begin    (* NumCnt *)

        Even := [4, 12, 16];
        Odd := [1, 7, 15]

    end.    (* NumCnt *)
    ```

PROGRAMMING PROBLEMS

1.   When searching large lists of records, sometimes several arrays of the same records will be maintained. Each array will contain all the records but will be sorted by a different key field. Write a program that allows the user to enter a list of employee records (there will not be more than 100 records). Each record should contain the following fields:

Name (maximum of 30 characters)
Social security number (XXX-XX-XXXX)
Sex (F/M)
Date hired (XX/XX/XX)

The program should store these records in two arrays: one sorted by name, the other by social security number. Then allow the user to locate a particular record by entering either the name or the social security number. A binary search should be used to search the appropriate array and display the contents of the specified record.

2.   Write a program to determine if a particular senior's choice of classes meets the minimum requirements at Bowsher High School. Each student must take five courses with at least one of the courses in each area below:

Course Number	Area	Course
101	English	English Literature
102		Contemporary Literature
103		Drama
104		Film Making
301	Math	Algebra II
302		Trigonometry
303		Calculus
304		Statistics
401	Science	Geology
402		Physics
403		Chemistry

Have the user enter the numbers of the five courses being taken by a student. Assign these numbers to a set and then use the set operators to determine if the student is taking at least one course in each of the three areas.

Chapter 12

Recursion and Sorting and Searching Algorithms

CHAPTER OBJECTIVES

After studying this chapter, you should be able to:

1. Define the term recursion and explain how recursive algorithms work.
2. Use recursion when appropriate in programs.
3. Explain how the insertion, selection, and merge sorts work.
4. Explain how the recursive quicksort works.
5. Write sorting procedures that use the insertion, selection, merge, and quick sorts.
6. Compare the efficiency of the different sorting algorithms.
7. Explain what is meant by "Big-O notation."
8. Explain how the binary search works and use it in programs when appropriate.
9. Explain what is meant by hashing.
10. Compare the efficiency of the different searching algorithms.

KEY TERMS

Collision The situation that occurs when a hashing routine gives the same result for two or more different key fields.

Embedded recursion A recursive process in which all or part of the processing by the subprogram is done after the stopping point has been reached and returns have been made from each of the recursive calls.

Forward declaration Used when the programmer specifies a subprogram's name and parameter list in advance of the actual declaration. This allows the subprogram to be called before it is declared.

Hashing routine   A formula used on a key field in a record to generate an address (often an array index) at which that record will be stored.

Indirect recursion   A cycle of subprograms that recursively call each other.

Key field   A field in a record that is used to determine the location at which the record will be stored. Often this field is used as input to a hashing routine; the result identifies the storage location.

Recursion   The situation in which a procedure or function calls itself.

Searching   Looking through a list in an attempt to locate a target element.

Sorting   Arranging data in a specified order, such as from smallest to largest (for numeric data) or alphabetically (for character data).

Tail recursion   A recursive process in which all of the processing by a subprogram is done before making a recursive call to the next level.

REVIEW OF KEY TERMS

When a subprogram calls itself, _____ occurs. In
(1)

_____ recursion all or part of a subprogram's processing is done after the
(2)

stopping point has been reached whereas in _____ recursion the
(3)

subprogram's processing is done before a recursive call to the next level is made. An example of

_____ recursion is when two subprograms recursively call each other. If you
(4)

wish to call a subprogram before it is declared you can use a(n) _____
(5)

declaration. _____ is the process of arranging a list in a particular order,
(6)

whereas _____ is the process of locating a specified item in a list of items.
(7)

A(n) _____ algorithm manipulates a(n) _____ field in such
(8)   (9)

a way as to generate an address at which a particular record is located. If the same address is

generated for two or more different records, a(n) _____ has occurred.
(10)

MULTIPLE CHOICE

1. What happens if a recursive subprogram has no stopping point?
    a. The subprogram will never be called.
    b. The subprogram will continue executing indefinitely.
    c. The subprogram will execute only once.
    d. The compiler will generate a syntax error.

2. Which of the following recursive procedures obtain the same output as the *while/do* loop below?

```
procedure PrLetters (Ch : char);
begin   (* PrLetters *)
   while Ch < 'g' do
   begin
      write (Ch:4);
      Ch := succ (Ch)
   end   (* while *)
end;   (* PrLetters *)
```

a.
```
procedure PrLetters (Ch : char);
begin   (* PrLetters *)
   write (Ch:4);
   if Ch < 'f'
      then PrLetters (succ (Ch))
   end;   (* PrLetters *)
```

c.
```
procedure PreLetters (Ch : char);
begin   (* PrLetters *)
   if Ch < 'g'
      then PrLetters (succ(Ch));
   write (Ch:4)
end;   (* PrLetters *)
```

b.
```
procedure PrLetters (Ch : char);
begin   (* PrLetters *)
   write (Ch:4);
   if Ch < 'g'
     then PrLetters (succ(Ch))
   end;   (* PrLetters *)
```

d.
```
procedure PrLetters (Ch : char);
begin   (* PrLetters *)
   if Ch < 'f'
      then PrLetters (succ(Ch));
   write (Ch:4)
end;   (* PrLetters *)
```

3. Which of the following is a valid example of a forward declaration for the following procedure heading?

```
procedure FindIncome (* Income1, Income2 : real; var Net : real *);
```

a. `procedure FindIncome (Income1, Income2 : real; var Net : real);`

b. `procedure FindIncome; forward;`

c. `procedure FindIncome (Income1, Income2 : real; var Net : real); forward;`

d. `FindIncome; forward;`

4. The advantage of using a forward declaration is it allows _____.
    a. the computer to execute a subprogram more efficiently
    b. a subprogram to call itself recursively
    c. a subprogram to be called before it is defined
    d. two subprograms to be executed simultaneously

5. Which of the following statements describes how a selection sort works?
    a. Each array element is examined in turn and moved forward in the array until its correct position is found.
    b. The entire array is searched for the smallest element which is moved to the first array position, then the remaining portion of the array is searched for the second smallest element which is moved to the second array position, and so forth until the entire array has been sorted.
    c. The sort compares adjacent array elements and exchanges them if they are out of order. This process is repeated until the entire array is examined without any exchanges being made.
    d. The sort orders a list by repeatedly partitioning the list, and choosing a pivot point. All elements larger than the pivot point are placed on one side of it and elements smaller than it are placed on the other side. This partitioning and switching process continues until each of the sublists has a length of one.

6. Which of the following statements describes how a bubble sort works?
    a. Each array element is examined in turn and moved forward in the array until its correct position is found.
    b. The entire array is searched for the smallest element which is moved to the first array position, then the remaining portion of the array is searched for the second smallest element which is moved to the second array position, and so forth until the entire array has been sorted.
    c. The sort compares adjacent array elements and exchanges them if they are out of order. This process is repeated until the entire array is examined without any exchanges being made.
    d. The sort orders a list by repeatedly partitioning the list, and choosing a pivot point. All elements larger than the pivot point are placed on one side of it and elements smaller than it are placed on the other side. This partitioning and switching process continues until each of the sublists has a length of one.

7. If a sequential search is used, how many items will have been examined by the time the value 28 is found?

    1   5   9   12   18   20   25   26   28   32   40
    a. 10   c. 6
    b. 5   d. 9

8. If a binary search is used, how many items will have been examined by the time the value 18 is found?

    1   5   9   12   18   20   25   26   28   32   40
    a. 2   c. 4
    b. 3   d. 5

9. A disadvantage of using a binary search is _____.
    a. the list must already be in order
    b. the list may not contain more than 50 items
    c. it cannot be used with a list containing character data
    d. it takes more computer time than searching algorithms such as the sequential search

10. If a bank wanted to produce a single listing of all customers by combining two sorted lists of savings and checking account customers, which of the algorithms listed below probably would be most efficient?

    a. bubble sort
    b. quicksort
    c. selection sort
    d. merge sort

11. Why is the middle value in a list a good choice for the pivot point in the quicksort?

    a. The computer is able to execute the quicksort faster if the middle value is used.
    b. If the list is already in order (or somewhat in order) the sorting process will be faster if the middle value is used.
    c. It makes the sorting process easier for people to understand.
    d. The middle value is not a good choice for the pivot point.

12. Which expression listed below states the number of comparisons needed when using a selection sort?

    a. $N * (N-1) / 2$
    b. $N^2 * (N-1) / 2$
    c. $(N - 1) / 2$
    d. $N * \log_2 N$

13. Which of the following algorithms uses a method similar to that you would use when efficiently locating a name in a telephone book?

    a. quick search
    b. binary search
    c. bubble sort
    d. sequential search

14. When using hash-coded searching, why is it necessary that each record in the list has a key field?

    a. The records are stored in ascending order according to the value stored in the key field.
    b. The hashing routine is applied to the value stored in the key field to determine where the record will be stored.
    c. The key field is used to sort the records.
    d. The key field contains the address at which the record is stored.

15. Under what condition will the following merge sort not work properly when merging the sorted arrays **X** and **Y** into array **Z**?

```
Count1 := 1;
Count2 := 1;
Count3 := 1;
while (Count1 <= Size1) and (Count2 <= Size2) do
begin
    if X[Count1] < Y[Count2]
        then
        begin
            Z[Count3] := X[Count1];
            Count1 := Count1 + 1
        end   (* then *)
        else
        begin
            Z[Count3] := Y[Count2];
            Count2 := Count2 + 1
        end;  (* else *)
        Count3 := Count3 + 1
end;   (* while *)

while Count1 < Size1 do
begin
    Z[Count3] := X[Count1];
    Count1 := Count1 + 1;
    Count3 := Count3 + 1
end   (* while *)
```

a. on lists of less than 10 elements
b. when the two lists to be merged are already ordered
c. when there are still some array elements remaining in **X** after **Y** has been merged into **Z**
d. when there are still some array elements remaining in **Y** after **X** has been merged into **Z**

ASSIGNMENTS

Assignment 1

Identify each of the sorting processes listed in parts a through d as one of the following:

bubble sort
selection sort
insertion sort
quicksort

a.	17	5	12	8	3	10
	5	17	12	8	3	10
	5	12	17	8	3	10
	5	8	12	17	3	10
	3	5	8	12	17	10
	3	5	8	10	12	17

_____

b.	17	5	12	8	3	10
	5	12	8	3	10	17
	5	8	3	10	12	17
	5	3	8	10	12	17
	3	5	8	10	12	17
	3	5	8	10	12	17

_____

c.	17	5	12	8	3	10
	3	5	12	8	17	10
	3	5	12	8	17	10
	3	5	8	12	17	10
	3	5	8	10	17	12
	3	5	8	10	12	17

_____

d.	17	5	12	8	3	10
	10	5	12	8	3	17
	10	5	3	8	12	17
	3	5	10	8	12	17
	3	5	8	10	12	17

_____

Assignment 2

This exercise provides a comparison of times needed for binary as compared to sequential searches. First perform the calculations necessary to fill in the following table. You need to determine the maximum amount of time necessary to perform the type of search specified. Note that column 2 contains the length of time the system takes to examine a specific element. The length of time is longer for the binary search because it has to perform the partitioning process in addition to comparing the element to the target. What generalized conclusions can you draw from this information?

Number of List Elements	Time Per Comparison (in microseconds)	Type of Search	Maximum Time to Locate Target (in microseconds)
8	1.5	Sequential	
8	12	Binary	
30	1.5	Sequential	
30	12	Binary	
300	1.5	Sequential	
300	12	Binary	
500	1.5	Sequential	
500	12	Binary	

DEBUGGING EXERCISES

Identify and correct the errors in the following program segments.

1.  ```pascal
    program Sort (Input, output);
    ```

    (* This program will read in a list of numbers, store them in an array,
    and then sort them from the smallest to the largest using procedure
    FastSort. *)

    ```pascal
    const
        Start = 1;
        Finish = 50;

    var
        List : array [Start..Finish] of integer;
        Num, I : integer;

    procedure FastSort (First, Last : integer);

    var
        L, R, Pivot, Temp : integer;

    begin     (* FastSort *)

        L := First;
        R := Last;
        Pivot := List[(First + Last) div 2];
        repeat
            while List[R] > Pivot do
                R := R - 1;
            while List[L] < Pivot do
                L := L + 1;
            if L <= R
                then
                begin
                    Temp := List[L];
                    List[L] := List[R];
                    List[R] := Temp;
                    L := L + 1;
                    R := R - 1
                end   (* if *)
        until L >= R;
        if First < R then FastSort (R, First);
        if L < Last then FastSort (L, Last)

    end;  (* FastSort *)

    begin  (* main *)

        writeln ('Enter a series of less than 50 numbers: ');
        Num := Start;
        while (not eoln) and (Num <= Finish) do
        begin
            read (List[Num]);
            Num := Num + 1
        end;  (* while *)
        Num := Num - 1;
        FastSort (Start, Num);
        for I := Start to Num do
            writeln (List[I])

    end.  (* main *)
    ```

2.  ```pascal
    function Power (I : real; J : integer) : real;

    begin

        Power := I * Power (I, J - 1)

    end;   (* Power *)
    ```

PROGRAMMING PROBLEMS

1.   One method of improving the efficiency of the quicksort is to alter it so that when the sublists become smaller than a specified value, a different sorting algorithm is used. For example, generally speaking the bubble sort is more efficient than the quicksort when used with lists containing fewer than 20 elements. Write a recursive quicksort procedure that will call a bubble sort to sort a sublist if its length is less than 20.

2.   One method of converting a base 10 number to base 2 is by using the division remainder method. In the example below, the base 10 number 14 is converted:

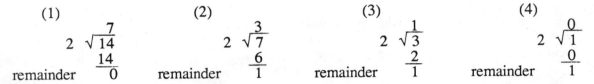

The remainders of the repeated division process are the digits 0111. In order to obtain the correct base 2 value the digits must be reversed to 1110. Write a program that will allow the user to enter a positive base 10 integer. A recursive procedure should then be called to convert this number to base 2. Each of the remainders should be placed in a successive element of an array. The array should then be output in reverse order to obtain the base 2 number.

Chapter 13

Pointer Variables and Linked Lists

CHAPTER OBJECTIVES

After studying this chapter, you should be able to:

1. Define and use dynamic variables and pointer variables.
2. Explain the difference between dynamic and static data structures.
3. Manipulate the contents of a node at any defined storage location.
4. Define and implement a linked list.
5. Write a procedure to insert a node into a linked list.
6. Write a procedure to delete a node from a linked list.
7. Use procedure *dispose* to free storage space.
8. Write a procedure to traverse a linked list.

KEY TERMS

Dynamic data structures A structure, consisting of a collection of elements, that can change in size depending on the data storage requirements of a program.

Dynamic variable A variable that may be created or disposed of as the program executes.

Linked list The simplest form of dynamic data structure, consisting of one or more nodes that are linked or connected together.

Multiply-linked list A list of elements, each having more than one link to another element.

Node An element in a dynamic data structure.

Pointer type The type of a pointer variable that may reference a particular type of storage location.

Pointer variable   A variable that contains the memory address of a dynamic variable.

Reference type   The particular type of variable that can be referenced by a pointer type.

Static data structure   A data structure that is declared at the beginning of a program or subprogram and remains in existence throughout the execution of the block in which it was declared. For each structure, the computer sets aside a small portion of its memory as a location.

Traverse   Traversing a linked list or tree involves following the pointers from node to node to retrieve information from the nodes.

REVIEW OF KEY TERMS

_____ data structures change in size during program execution whereas
(1)

_____ data structures stay the same size. A(n) _____ is a
(2)   (3)

dynamic data structure made up of nodes each of which points to the next node in the structure.

Each node contains a(n) _____ field which is the address of the next node in
(4)

the list. A linked list can be _____ from beginning to end by starting at the
(5)

_____ node and continuing until a node with a nil pointer is encountered.
(6)

MULTIPLE CHOICE

1. In dynamic data structures _____ .
   a. the amount of storage space needed by the structure is defined at the beginning of the program
   b. arrays are used to store data
   c. storage space for each node in the structure is allocated during program execution as it is needed
   d. individual nodes are referenced by using a subscript

2. Which of the following is *not* an advantage of using a dynamic data structure?
   a. They are easier for the programmer to define and manipulate than static data structures.
   b. The amount of memory space can vary depending on current needs.
   c. It is easier to insert a new element than it is in a static structure such as an array.
   d. It is easier to remove an element than it is in a static structure such as an array.

   Use the following program segment to answer Questions 3-9.

```
program BowlingScores (input, output);

type
   Ptr = ^BowlerNode;
   BowlerNode = record
      Number : integer;
      Ave : real
   end;   (* record *)

var
   Bowler1, Bowler2, Bowler3 : Ptr;

begin   (* BowlingScores *)

   new (Bowler1);
   Bowler1^.Number := 35;
   Bowler1^.Ave := 124.5
```

3. The pointer type(s) in this definition is/are _____ .
   a. BowlerNode
   b. Bowler
   c. Ptr
   d. Bowler1, Bowler2, Bowler3

4. The reference type(s) in this definition is/are _____ .
   a. BowlerNode
   b. Bowler
   c. Ptr
   d. Bowler1, Bowler2, Bowler3

5. The pointer variable(s) is/are _____ .
   a. BowlerNode
   b. Bowler
   c. Ptr
   d. Bowler1, Bowler2, Bowler3

6. Which of the following will assign the value 140.9 to the *Ave* field of **Bowler2**?
   a. Bowler2^.Ave := 140.9
   b. Ptr^.Bowler2^.Ave := 140.9
   c. Bowler2.Ave := 140.9
   d. Bowler2^.BowlerNode.Ave := 140.9

7. The purpose of the statement new (Bowler1) is to _____.
    a. assign values to the fields of node *Bowler1*
    b. set aside storage space for a node pointed to by *Bowler1*
    c. link the node *Bowler1* to the node in front of it
    d. delete the node *Bowler1*

8. What effect does the statement "Bowler2 := Bowler1" have?
    a. It copies the values of the fields stored in *Bowler1* into *Bowler2*. The addresses in the respective pointer variables remain unchanged.
    b. It has no effect on either *Bowler1* or *Bowler2*.
    c. It copies the address stored in *Bowler1* into *Bowler2* so that both pointers now point to the same location.
    d. It creates an empty node pointed to by *Bowler2*.

9. What effect does the following have?
    ```
    new (Bowler3);
    Bowler3^ := Bowler1^
    ```
    a. It copies the values of the fields stored in *Bowler1* into *Bowler3*. The addresses in the respective pointer variables remain unchanged.
    b. It has no effect on either *Bowler1* or *Bowler3*.
    c. It copies the address stored in *Bowler1* into *Bowler3* so that both pointers now point to the same location.
    d. It creates an empty node pointed to by *Bowler3*.

Use the following program segment to answer Questions 10-14.

```
type
    DayRange = 1..7;
    TimeRange = 1..24;

FlightPtr = ^FlightRec;
FlightRec = record
    Num : Integer;
    Day : DayRange;
    Time : TimeRange;
    Link : FlightPtr
end;   (* record *)

var
    Head, Next, Last : FlightPtr;
    I : Integer;

begin

    new (Head);
    Next := Head;
    for I := 1 to 5 do
    begin
        Next^.Link := nil;
        write ('Enter the flight number: ');
        readln (Next^.Num);
        write ('Enter the flight day: ');
        readln (Next^.Day);
        write ('Enter the flight time: ');
        readln (Next^.Time);
        Last := Next;
        new (Next);
        Last^.Link := Next
    end   (* for *)
```

10. This node has _____ data field(s) and _____ pointer field(s).
    a. 1, 3
    b. 4, 0
    c. 3, 1
    d. 0, 4

11. The purpose of the pointer *Head* is to _____.
    a. indicate the end of the list
    b. point to the first node in the list
    c. assign values to a new node's list
    d. link the current node to the last node

12. The purpose of the statement "Next^.Link := nil" is to _____.
    a. indicate the location of the first node in the list
    b. make certain that the *Link* field of the last node in the list has a value of *nil*
    c. make sure that each node in the list points to the next node
    d. make sure that each node in the list points to the previous node

13. The statement which links the previous node to the current node is _____.
    a. Next^.Link := nil
    b. Last := Next
    c. new (Next)
    d. Last^.Link := Next

14. In this program segment each new node is inserted _____.
    a. at the beginning of the list
    b. at the end of the list
    c. into the list in numerical order according to the value of the *Num* field
    d. randomly into the list

ASSIGNMENTS

Assignment 1

Draw a diagram that would illustrate the nodes that **M, N, O,** and **P** are pointing to after execution of the following program segment.

```
type
    SportType = (Soccer, Baseball, Hockey, Tennis, Swimming, Golf);
    Pointer = ^SportType;

var
    M, N, O, P : Pointer;

begin

    new (M);
    M^ := Baseball;
    new (P);
    P^ := pred (Tennis);
    new (O);
    O^ := Swimming;
    N := M;
    P^ := M^;
    P^ := succ (Swimming);
    N^ := Soccer
```

COMPUTER SCIENCE WITH PASCAL

Assignment 2

Using the following program segment, explain the purpose of each of the numbered statements listed in the table.

Purpose

```program ListCreation (input, output);```
```type```
```   MonthRange = 0..12;```
```1. Pointer = ^MonthNode;```
	1.

```2. MonthNode = record```
```   Month : MonthRange;```
```   Precip : real;```
```   AveTemp : real;```
	2.

```3.   Link : Pointer```
```   end;   (* MonthNode *)```
``` var```
	3.

```4. First, Next : Pointer;```
```   Counter : integer;```
```(***)```
``` procedure CreateNode (var Next : Pointer);```
``` var```
```   Temp : Pointer;```
	4.

```begin   (* CreateNode *)```
```   new (Temp);```
```5. Next^.Link := Temp;```
	5.

Assignment 2 (cont.)

Purpose

```
6.    Next := Temp;
      write ('Enter integer representing month: ');
      readln (Next^.Month);
      write ('Enter amount of precipitation: ');
      readln (Next^.Precip);
      write ('Enter average temperature: ');
      readln (Next^.AveTemp);
7.    Next^.Link := nil
   end;   (* CreateNode *)
   (********************************************)
   begin   (* main *)
      new (First);
8.    First^.Month := 0;
      First^.Link := nil;
      Next := First;
      for Counter := 1 to 12 do
         CreateNode (Next)
   end.   (* main *)
```

6.

7.

8.

DEBUGGING EXERCISES

Identify and correct the errors in the following programs and program segments.

1.
```
(* This segment reads a search value and traverses a linked list
   looking for a match. *)

type
   Product = record
      CodeNum : integer;
      Price : integer
   end;  (* Product *)
   ProductPointer = ^Product;
   ProductNode = record
      ProductInfo : Product;
      Next : ProductPointer
   end;  (* ProductNode *)

var
   Head : ProductPointer;

(*****************************************************************)

procedure FindNode (Head : ProductPointer);

var
   SearchCode : integer;
   LastNode, SearchNode : ProductPointer;

begin (* FindNode *)

   readln (SearchCode);
   SearchNode := Head;

   while (SearchNode^.ProductInfo.CodeNum <> SearchCode)
         and (SearchNode^.Next <> nil) do
   begin
      LastNode := SearchNode;
      SearchNode := SearchNode^.Next
   end;  (* while *)

   if SearchNode^.ProductInfo.CodeNum = SearchCode
      then writeln (SearchNode^.Price)

end;  (* FindNode *)
```

2.
```
program FillNode (input);

(* Create and fill a node. *)

type
   Node = record
      OrderNum : integer;
      Quantity : integer
   end;  (* Node *)
   Pointer = ^Node;

var
   OrderNode : Pointer;

begin  (* FillNode *)

   readln (OrderNode^.OrderNum);
   readln (OrderNode^.Quantity)

end.   (* FillNode *)
```

PROGRAMMING PROBLEMS

1.   The Klingons have captured Spock, science officer of the U.S.S. Enterprise. Captain Kirk has broken into their prison colony to free him. He has reached the computer that possesses information concerning all of the prisoners, including their cell numbers. Write a program to store the data in a linked list and print information regarding a prisoner when his or her name is entered.

2.   Create a linked list that contains nodes of the type defined in Assignment #1 in Chapter 11. Arrange the list so that the records are maintained in order by player number. Allow the user to search the linked list for a particular player's record and display it with appropriate labels.

Chapter 14

Stacks and Queues

CHAPTER OBJECTIVES

After studying this chapter, you should be able to:

1. Define a stack.
2. Implement a stack as an array.
3. Implement a stack as a linked list.
4. Write the code necessary to pop items off and push items on to a stack.
5. Define a queue.
6. Implement a queue as a linked list.
7. Write the code necessary to add or delete elements from a queue.

KEY TERMS

Circular definition   A declaration of a new pointer type that points to a record is circular, because it must use the record type as its reference type in the pointer declaration before the record type has been defined. The pointer type is then used inside the record declaration to complete the definition.

Pop   To remove the topmost node on a stack.

Push   To insert a node at the top of a stack.

Queue   A list in which all insertions are made at the end of the list, and all deletions are made from the beginning.

Stack   A list in which all insertions and deletions take place at one end, called the *top*.

REVIEW OF KEY TERMS

A(n) _____ is a structure in which the first element inserted is the first
$\qquad$ (1)

deleted whereas a(n) _____ is a structure in which the first item inserted is the
$\qquad$ (2)

last item deleted. When a node is removed from the top of a stack it is _____
$\qquad$ (3)

off and when a node is added to a stack it is _____ on. A(n)
$\qquad$ (4)

_____ list is a queue in which head and tail are connected.
$\qquad$ (5)

MULTIPLE CHOICE

1. Which of the following is an example of a stack?
    a. The grocery store check-out.
    b. Programs waiting to be executed by the computer system.
    c. Dishes in a cupboard.
    d. Students waiting to sign up for a course.

2. Which of the following is the fairest way of allotting tickets to a rock concert?
    a. by using a queue   c. by using a deque
    b. by using a stack   d. by using a node

Use the following diagram and program segment to answer Questions 3-7.

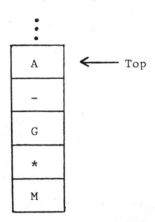

```
type
    Range = 1..100;
    StackType = record
        Elements : array[Range] of char;
        Top : Range
    end;    (* StackType *)

var
    Stack : StackType;
```

3. If all of the values on this stack were popped off and printed in the order they were popped,
    the result would be _____.
    a. A - G * M   c. A * G - M
    b. M * G - A   d. M - A * G

4. This is an example of a stack being implemented as a(n) _____.
    a. linked list   c. array
    b. node   d. queue

5. What is the maximum number of elements that can be on this stack at one time?
   a. As many as can be stored in the computer's memory.
   b. 100
   c. 5
   d. It depends on the current position of *Top*.

6. Assuming that procedure *Pop* pops the top element off *Stack* and places it in its argument and *Push* pushes its argument onto *Stack*, what will the values of **X** and **Y** be after this program segment is executed?

   ```
   Pop (X);
   Push ('/');
   Pop (X);
   Push ('Y');
   Pop (Y);
   Pop (Y)
   ```

   a. X = '/', Y = '-'   c. X = '-', Y = 'Y'
   b. X = 'A', Y = '-'   d. X = 'Y', Y = '/'

7. Which of the following defines a linked list that could be used to implement the stack illustrated above?

   a.
   ```
   type
       StackPointer = ^StackType;
       StackType = record
          Value : char
       end;   (* StackType *)

   var
       Top : StackPointer;
   ```

   c.
   ```
   type
       StackPointer = ^StackType;
       StackPointer = record
          Value : char;
          Link : StackPointer
       end;   (* StackType *)

   var
       Top : StackPointer;
   ```

   b.
   ```
   type
       StackPointer = ^StackType;
       StackType = record
          Value  : char;
          Link : StackPointer
       end;   (* StackType *)

   var
       Top : StackType;
   ```

   d.
   ```
   type
       StackPointer = ^StackType;
       StackType = record
          Value : char;
          Link : StackPointer
       end;   (* StackType *)

   var
       Top : StackPointer;
   ```

Use the following illustration to answer Questions 8 and 9.

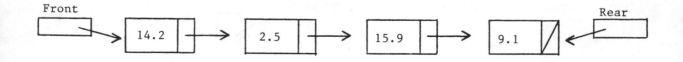

8. Each node in this queue has _____ field(s) and _____ field(s).
    a. two data, no pointer
    b. two pointer, no data
    c. one data, two pointer
    d. one data, one pointer

9. Which of the following defines a linked list that could be used to represent this queue?

    a.
    ```
    type
        QueuePointer = ^QueueRec;
        QueueRec = record
          RNum : real;
          Link : QueueRec
        end;   (* QueueRec *)

    var
        Front, Rear : QueuePointer;
    ```

    c.
    ```
    type
        QueuePointer = ^Link;
        QueueRec = record
          RNum : real;
          Link : QueuePointer
        end;   (* QueueRec *)

    var
        Front, Rear : QueuePointer;
    ```

    b.
    ```
    type
        QueuePointer = ^QueueRec;
        QueueRec = record
          RNum : real;
          Link : QueuePointer
        end;   (* QueueRec *)

    var
        Front, Rear : QueuePointer;
    ```

    d.
    ```
    type
        QueuePointer^ = QueueRec;
        QueueRec = record
          RNum : real;
          Link : QueuePointer
        end;   (* QueueRec *)

    var
        Front, Rear : QueuePointer;
    ```

10. In a deque _____.
    a. deletions always are made from the front and insertions to the rear
    b. deletions and insertions always are made at the bottom
    c. both deletions and insertions can be made at either end
    d. deletions are always made from the rear and insertions to the front

11. When implementing a linked list as a deque each node must have _____.
    a. two forward pointers
    b. two backward pointers
    c. a single forward pointer
    d. a forward and a backward pointer

12. The advantage of using a circular list is _____.
    a. only a single pointer can be used to point to both the front and the rear
    b. there is no need for each node to have a pointer field
    c. it is identical to a stack
    d. There is no advantage to using a circular list.

ASSIGNMENTS

Assignment 1

Several of the statements in procedures *Push* and *Pop* are out of order. Place them in the correct order.

```
type
   DayType = (Sunday, Monday, Tuesday, Wednesday, Thursday,
              Friday, Saturday);
   StackPointer = ^CustomersNode;
   CustomersNode = record
     Day : DayType;
     Customers : Integer;
     Link : StackPointer
   end;    (* CustomersNode *)

var
   Top : StackPointer;
   DayValue : DayType;
   CustomerValue : Integer;

(**********************************************************)

procedure Push (var Top : StackPointer; DayValue : Daytype;
                CustomerValue : Integer);

var
   Hold : StackPointer;

begin    (* Push *)

   Top := Hold;
   Hold^.Day := DayValue;
   Hold^.Customers := CustomerValue;
   new (Hold)

end;    (* Push *)

(**********************************************************)

procedure Pop (var Top : StackPointer; var DayValue :
               DayType; var CustomerValue : Integer);

var
   Hold : StackPointer;

(* * * * * * * * * * * * * * * * * * * * * * * * * * * *)

function Empty (Top : StackPointer) : boolean;

begin    (* Empty *)

   If Top = nil
      then Empty := true
      else Empty := false

end;    (* Empty *)

(* * * * * * * * * * * * * * * * * * * * * * * * * * * *)
```

Assignment 1 (cont.)

```
begin    (* Pop *)

    if Empty (Top)
        then writeln ('The stack is empty.')
        else
        begin
            Top := Top^.Link;
            CustomerValue := Top^.Customer;
            Hold := Top;
            DayValue :=  Top^.Day;
            dispose (Hold)
        end    (* else *)

end;    (* Pop *)
```

Assignment 2

Draw an illustration showing how the queue created by the following program segment will look after the segment is executed.

```
program MakeQueue (Input, output);

type
    DayType = (Sunday, Monday, Tuesday, Wednesday, Thursday,
               Friday, Saturday);

QueuePointer = ^CustomersNode;
CustomersNode = record
    Day : DayType;
    Customers : Integer;
    Link : QueuePointer
end;   (* CustomersNode *)

var
    Front, Rear, Last, Temp : QueuePointer;

begin   (* MakeQueue *)

    new (Front);
    Front^.Day := Monday;
    Front^.Customers := 302;
    Front^.Link := nil;
    Last := Front;

    new (Temp);
    Temp^.Day := Friday;
    Temp^.Customers := 254;
    Temp^.Link := nil;
    Last^.Link := Temp;
    Last := Temp;

    new (Temp);
    Temp^.Day := Saturday;
    Temp^.Customers := 182;
    Temp^.Link := nil;
    Last^.Link := Temp;
    Last := Temp;

    new (Temp);
    Temp^.Day := Saturday;
    Temp^.Customers := 182;
    Temp^.Link := nil;
    Last^.Link := Temp;
    Last := Temp;

    Front := Front^.Link;

    new (Temp);
    Temp^.Day := pred (Wednesday);
    Temp^.Customers := 238;
    Temp^.Link := nil;
    Last^.Link := Temp;
    Last := Temp;
    Rear := Last

end.
```

DEBUGGING EXERCISES

Identify and correct the errors in the following program segments.

1.
```
procedure Pop (Top : StkPtr; Number : real);

(* Procedure to pop a real number off of a stack implemented as a linked
   list.  The number is then returned to the calling program.        *)

var
    Temp : StkPtr;

begin   (* Pop *)

    if Top <> nil
       then
       begin
          Number := Top^.Num;
          Temp := Top;
          Top := Top^ - 1
       end
       else writeln ('Stack is empty')

end;  (* Pop *)
```

2.
```
program JobQueue (input, output);

    type
        JobQPtr : ^JobNode;
        JobNode = record
            JobNumber : integer;
            Link : JobQPtr
        end;  (* JobNode *)

    var
        Front, Rear : JobQPtr;
        NextJob : integer;

    procedure DeQue (var NextJob : integer);

    (* Removes first job number from queue *)

    var
        Temp : JobQPtr;

    begin

        if Front = nil
           then writeln ('Job queue is empty')
        else
        begin
           NextJob := Front^.JobNumber;
           Temp := Rear;
           Front := Front^.Link;
           dispose (Temp);
           if Front = nil
              then Rear := nil
        end   (* if *)

    end;  (* DeQue *)
```

PROGRAMMING PROBLEMS

1.   A common problem in writing nested expressions is the improper use of parentheses. Write a procedure that will read an expression and determine if there is a right parenthesis for each left parenthesis. Use a stack to keep track. Whenever a left parenthesis is encountered, it should be pushed on the stack. When a right parenthesis is encountered, a left parenthesis should be popped off the stack. Have the procedure display an appropriate message.

2.   Write a non-recursive quicksort. This can be accomplished by placing the subscripts of the portions of the array that still need to be manipulated on a stack. When it is time to manipulate a particular portion of the array, the needed subscripts can be popped off the stack.

Chapter 15

Trees

CHAPTER OBJECTIVES

After studying this chapter, you should be able to:

1. Define a tree.
2. Explain the difference between an ordered and a nonordered tree.
3. Define and correctly use the terminology associated with trees.
4. List the characteristics of a binary tree.
5. Write a program to create a binary tree.
6. List the steps in each of the three types of tree traversals.
7. Write the code necessary to perform each of the three types of tree traversals.
8. Write the code necessary to add a node to a binary tree.
9. Write the code necessary to delete a node from a binary tree.

KEY TERMS

Ancestor   A node on the path from a given node to the root.

Binary tree   A dynamic data structure that may connect a maximum of two child nodes to a single parent node via two different pointers. In turn, two more nodes may be connected to each of these two added nodes. This process continues until leaves are formed. Binary trees are ordered trees.

Branch   A statement used to alter the normal flow of program execution.

Child   A node immediately below a parent node in a tree.

Descendant   Any node that comes below a given node in a tree.

Leaf node   In a tree, a node that has no children.

Non-ordered tree   A tree in which the relative positions of the subtrees are not significant.

Ordered tree   A tree in which the relative positions of the subtrees are significant. A binary tree is an ordered tree.

Parent   In a tree, a node that has a branch or branches to other nodes.

Root node   On particular node at the top of a tree structure; it has no parent and is the ancestor to all other nodes.

Siblings   Children of the same parent node.

Subtree   A portion of a tree, consisting of one node called the *root*, and its descendants, if any. A subtree is also a tree.

Tree   A dynamic data stucture that has one or more nodes. One node is designated as the root, which points to zero or more distinct subtrees.

Visit   Perform some operation, such as retrieval of data, on a node.

REVIEW OF KEY TERMS

A(n) _____ is a nonlinear data structure with one or more nodes one of
              (1)

which is designated as the _____ which contains branches to one or more
                                    (2)

_____. Tree terminology is much like that of a family tree. A(n)
       (3)

_____ node can have one or more children which are
       (4)

_____ to each other. Any node between a given node and the root is that
       (5)

node's ancestor. When a linked list is implemented as a tree, the _____
                                                                            (6)

contain the pointers to the next nodes. If the branches of a node are all nil, the node is a(n)

_____. In a(n) _____ tree the relative positions of the
       (7)   (8)

subtrees are significant whereas in a(n) _____ tree they are not. A(n)
                                                  (9)

_____ tree is an ordered tree that can contain zero or more subtrees; each node
       (10)

may have a maximum of two children. When a node in a tree is _____, some
                                                                        (11)

operation, such as reading its fields, is performed on the node.

MULTIPLE CHOICE

1. Which of the following is *not* true of a tree?
   a. One node must be designated as the root.
   b. The root node points to one or more subtrees.
   c. Each node can have no more than two children.
   d. It is a nonlinear data structure.

2. The difference between an ordered tree and a nonordered tree is _____.
   a. A nonordered tree can be empty whereas an ordered tree must have at least one node.
   b. In a nonordered tree the relative positions of the subtrees are significant whereas in an ordered tree they are not significant.
   c. In an ordered tree the relative positions of the subtrees are significant whereas in a nonordered tree they are not significant.
   d. An ordered tree has a root node whereas a nonordered tree does not.

3. Which of the following is not included in the definition of a binary tree?
   a. A binary tree can have a maximum of 10 levels.
   b. A binary tree can have zero or more subtrees.
   c. Each node can have no more than two branches.
   d. The relative positions of the subtrees are significant.

   Use the following binary tree to answer Questions 4-9.

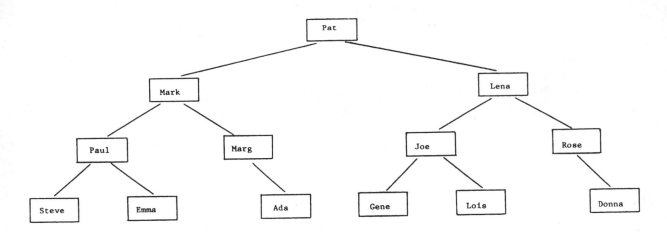

4. How many levels does this binary tree have?
   a. 1
   b. 13
   c. 2
   d. 4

5. Marg is a _____ of Mark.
   a. child
   b. parent
   c. sibling
   d. ancestor

6. Marg is a _____ of Paul.
   a. child
   b. parent
   c. sibling
   d. ancestor

7. This tree has _____ leaves.
   a. 8
   b. 13
   c. 15
   d. 6

8. Which of the following nodes is not an ancestor of Steve?
   a. Pat
   b. Mark
   c. Paul
   d. Emma

9. An inorder traversal of this tree will result in the nodes being visited in which of the following orders?
   a. Pat Mark Paul Steve Emma Marg Ada Lena Joe Gene Lois Rose Donna
   b. Steve Paul Emma Mark Marg Ada Pat Gene Joe Lois Lena Rose Donna
   c. Steve Emma Paul Ada Marg Mark Gene Lois Joe Donna Rose Lena
   d. Steve Paul Emma Mark Ada Marg Pat Gene Joe Lois Lena Donna Rose

10. A full binary tree with 7 levels can have a maximum of _____ leaves.
    a. 16
    b. 32
    c. 64
    d. 128

11. If the root of a binary tree is considered level 1, what is the maximum number of nodes that a tree with 7 levels can have?
    a. 63
    b. 64
    c. 127
    d. 254

Use the following program segment to answer Questions 12-15.

```
type
   Branch = ^Tree;
   Tree = record
      Person : packed array[1..20] of char;
      Birth : packed array[1..10] of char;
      Left, Right : Branch
   end;   (* Tree *)

var
   Root : Branch;
```

12. Each node in this tree can have _____.
    a. a maximum of one child
    b. a maximum of two children
    c. a maximum of three children
    d. any number of children

13. Which of the following procedures will perform a preorder traversal of the above binary tree?

a.
```
procedure Traverse (Root : Branch);

begin   (* Traverse *)

   If Root <> nil
      then
      begin
         Traverse (Root^.Left);
         writeln (Root^.Person);
         Traverse (Root^.Right);
      end   (* then *)

   end;   (* Traverse *)
```

c.
```
procedure Traverse (Root : Branch);

begin   (* Traverse *)

   If Root <> nil
      then
      begin
         Traverse (Root^.Left);
         Traverse (Root^.Right);
         writeln (Root^.Person)
      end   (* then *)

   end;   (* Traverse *)
```

b.
```
procedure Traverse (Root : Branch);

begin   (* Traverse *)

   If Root <> nil
      then
      begin
         writeln (Root^.Person);
         Traverse (Root^.Left);
         Traverse (Root^.Right)
      end   (* then *)

   end;   (* Traverse *)
```

d.
```
procedure Traverse (Root : Branch);

begin   (* Traverse *)

   If Root <> nil
      then
      begin
         writeln (Root^.Person);
         Traverse (Root^.Left)
      end   (* then *)

   end;   (* Traverse *)
```

14. The basic reason that it is easier to add a node to a binary tree than to delete one is _____.
   a. new nodes are always added as leaves
   b. new nodes are always added at the root
   c. new nodes always have two subtrees
   d. there is no reason

15. Which of the following is not a situation that must be dealt with when removing a node from a binary tree?
   a. The situation in which the node is a leaf.
   b. The situation in which the node has one subtree.
   c. The situation in which the node has two subtrees.
   d. The situation in which the node has three or more subtrees.

ASSIGNMENTS

Assignment 1

Fill in the table on page 267 using the tree below. In addition, answer the following questions.

a. How many subtrees does A have? What are the roots of each tree?

b. How many subtrees does each of the subtrees of A have? Draw boxes around all of the subtrees in the tree.

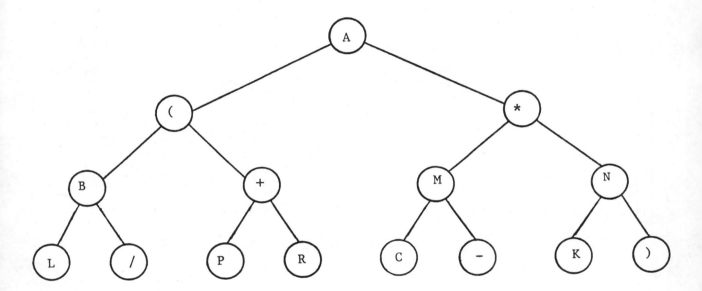

Assignment 1 (cont.)

Question	Answer
Number of leaf nodes	
Number of internal (non-leaf) nodes	
Height of the tree	
Which levels are filled?	
Values output by a preorder traversal	
Values output by an inorder traversal	

Assignment 2

Create binary trees from the following lists of letters such that an inorder traversal of each tree will result in the letters being visited in alphabetical order.

a. L   R   S   A   Q   P   B

b. B   Q   R   Z   L   J   M   T

c. O   W   C   V   F   P   R   S   A

d. M   Q   X   K   G   F   C   A

DEBUGGING EXERCISES

Identify and correct the errors in the following program segments.

```pascal
program MakeTree (input, output);

type
   Branch = ^TreeNode;
   TreeNode = record
      Item : char;
      L, R : Branch
   end;   (* TreeNode *)

var
   Root : Branch;
```

1.
```pascal
procedure Preorder (Root : Branch);
(* Performs a preorder traversal of the tree pointed to by Root. *)

begin
   If Root <> nil
      then
      begin
         writeln (Root^.Item:3);
         Preorder (Root^.R);
         Preorder (Root^.L)
      end   (* then *)
end;   (* Preorder *)
```

2.
```pascal
begin
(* Create a root node. *)

   new (Root);
   Root^.Item := '*';
   Root.L := nil;
   Root.R := nil
```

PROGRAMMING PROBLEMS

1.   Read a file containing a list of customer records alphabetized by name. Each record contains the following fields:

Name
Transaction Amount

A binary tree should be created in which each node contains a customer's record. However, a given customer may have more than one record in the file. When this happens, create only one node for the customer. Add or subtract any transactions in subsequent records and place the resulting balance in the node's balance field. For example, Rebecca Couch has three records in the input file:

Rebecca Couch
195.42

Rebecca Couch
-82.30

Rebecca Couch
-10.50

The values of the data fields in the node added to the binary tree will be:

Rebecca Couch
102.62

2.   Write a program that will permit you to create your own family tree. Place yourself at the root and then add on as many generations of relatives as possible. Print the contents of the tree.

Chapter 16

Applications of Computing

CHAPTER OBJECTIVES

After studying this chapter, you should be able to:

1. Define each of the three categories into which software packages can be divided.
2. Give examples of productivity tools.
3. Give examples of functional tools.
4. Give examples of end-user development tools.
5. Explain how simulation software is developed.
6. Define expert systems.
7. Discuss how computers are used in business, science, and education.
8. Discuss some trends in the microcomputer field.
9. Explain how laser technology is used in fiber optics.
10. Describe and give some advantages of parallel processing.
11. Explain what is meant by artificial intelligence.

KEY TERMS

Artificial intelligence (AI)   Field of research currently developing techniques whereby computers can be used to solve problems that appear to require imagination, intuition, or intelligence.

Computer-aided design (CAD)   Process of designing, drafting, and analyzing a prospective product using computer graphics on a video terminal.

Computer-aided manufacturing (CAM)   Use of a computer to simulate or monitor the steps of a manufacturing process.

Computer literacy   General knowledge about computers; includes some technical knowledge about hardware and software, the ability to use computers to solve problems, and awareness of how computers affect society.

Computerized axial tomography (CAT) scanning   Form of noninvasive physical testing that combines x-ray techniques and computers to aid diagnosis.

Data-base management systems (DBMS)   A set of programs that serves as the interface between the data base and the programmer, operating system, and users; also programs used to design and maintain data bases.

Electronic funds transfer (EFT)   A cashless method of managing money; accounts involved in a transaction are adjusted by electronic communications between computers.

Electronic spreadsheet   An electronic ledger sheet used to store and manipulate any type of numeric data.

End-user development tools   Tools that allow the end-user to develop an application package, usually through the use of a fourth-generation programming language. Examples of end-user development tools are simulation software, statistical packages, and data-base management systems.

Expert system   Software designed to imitate the same decision-making and evaluation processes of experts in a specific field.

Fiber optics   A data transmission concept using laser pulses and cables made of tiny threads of glass that can transmit huge amounts of data at the speed of light.

Functional tools   A category of application software packages that perform specific tasks or functions, such as inventory control.

Modem   A device that modulates and demodulates signals transmitted over communication facilities.

Multiphasic health testing (MPHT)   Computer-assisted testing plan that compiles data on patients and their test results, which are compared with norms to aid the physician in making a diagnosis.

Nondestructive testing (NDT)   Testing done electronically to avoid breaking, cutting, or tearing apart a product to find a problem.

Optical scanner   A device used to read machine-readable codes such as UPCs.

Parallel processing   A type of processing in which instructions and data are handled simultaneously.

Point-of-sale (POS) terminals   An input device that records information at the point where a good is sold.

Productivity tools   Application software packages that can increase the productivity of the user. Examples are text processors and graphics packages.

Simulation software   Software that creates computer generated models based on the analysis of data.

Spelling checker Application software that checks words in a document against a dictionary file. Any words in the document that are not in the file are flagged. Spelling checkers are often included in text processing packages.

Statistical package A software package that performs statistical analysis of data. Examples are SAS, SPSS, and Minitab.

Telecommunication The combined use of communication facilities, such as telephone systems and data-processing equipment.

Terminal communication package Software that allows different computers to communicate usually across telephone lines.

Text processor An application software package that is used to create documents. Tasks such as correcting, editing, and manipulating text can be performed efficiently.

Universal Product Code (UPC) A machine-readable code consisting of thirty dark bars and twenty-nine spaces that identifies a product and its manufacturer; commonly used on most grocery items.

Word processor See **Text processor**.

REVIEW OF KEY TERMS

Application software can be divided into three broad categories: _____
(1)

tools which are designed to perform a specific task, _____ tools that help the
(2)

user in performing common tasks such as word processing, and _____ tools
(3)

that allow the user to easily develop software that meets his or her needs. Electronic

_____ contain ledger sheets and are used to manipulate numeric data.
(4)

_____ allow the user to easily enter text, edit it, and store it on disk for later
(5)

use. These packages often include _____ that compare each word in the text
(6)

to an on-line dictionary to catch any possible spelling mistakes. _____
(7)

software uses a model to project what is likely to happen in a particular situation.

_____ packages are used to analyze data through the use of statistics.
(8)

_____ attempt to mimic the decision-making of experts in a narrowly-defined
(9)

field such as oil prospecting. This software accesses a knowledge base to answer user

questions. Researchers hope to develop computers with _____ that would
(10)

have humanlike thinking, common sense and be able to learn from past experiences. Most items

in retail stores contain a(n) _____ which can be used by
(11)

_____ to record customer purchases similar to the manner in which a cash
(12)

register is used. The codes are read using a(n) _____. Many businesses and
(13)

industries use _____ to help in the development of new products. Software
(14)

called _____ can then be used to facilitate the actual manufacturing process. A
          (15)

term used in education, _____ , is generally defined as having a knowledge of
                (16)

the types of tasks computers can perform, basic hardware knowledge, and some experience with

application software such as word processors. A(n) _____ package is
                                    (17)

necessary to allow computers to pass data back and forth over phone lines. It is also necessary to

have an electronic device called a(n) _____ which converts the computer's
                          (18)

signals to a form that can be transmitted over telephone lines. _____ is a
                                          (19)

fairly new concept that involves dividing a program into several portions and then executing the

portions simultaneously.

MULTIPLE CHOICE

1. Which of the following is an example of a productivity tool?
   a. a data base management system
   b. a software package that calculates the payroll for a factory
   c. a statistical package
   d. a word processor

2. _____ software allows the user to create documents that are close to the quality of type-set documents and can contain different styles and sizes of type, sophisticated graphics, and so forth.
   s. Spreadsheet
   b. Desk-top publishing
   c. Word processing
   d. Data base

3. Which of the following is not an example of an end-user development tool?
   a. simulation software
   b. spreadsheets
   c. data-base management systems
   d. statistical packages

4. The software in functional tools often is divided into modules so that _____.
   a. different modules can be implemented depending on each user's needs
   b. it will execute more quickly
   c. it is easier to use
   d. it can perform accounting functions

5. Electronic spreadsheets are used to _____.
   a. perform accounting operations
   b. analyze statistical data
   c. output statistical results in graph form
   d. simulate real-life situations

6. Which of the following is not a function commonly performed by word processors?
   a. They allow the user to correct typing mistakes.
   b. They allow sections of text to be moved or deleted.
   c. They allow text to be sent over telephone lines.
   d. They allow new text to be inserted as needed.

7. Expert systems use _____ to determine the answer to questions posed by users.
   a. simulation
   b. knowledge bases
   c. statistical packages
   d. data-base management systems

8. If you needed software that could determine the average, range, standard deviation, and so forth, of a collection of research data, you would need a _____.
   a. spreadsheet
   b. word processor
   c. expert system
   d. statistical package

9. The purpose of point-of-sale terminals is to _____.
   a. provide a model of what will happen in a particular situation
   b. read the bar code that is present on most retail merchandise and use this information to determine the item's price, update inventory, and so forth
   c. send data over telephone lines
   d. help automate the manufacturing process

10. A software package that could project the amount of damage that would be caused by a hypothetical earthquake is an example of _____ software.
   a. functional
   b. graphic
   c. simulation
   d. data-base

11. Fiber optics uses _____ to quickly and accurately carry signals through hair-thin glass fibers.
   a. a modem
   b. telecommunication packages
   c. parallel processing
   d. lasers

12. _____ use(s) computers to control x-ray machines and provide physicians with three-dimensional composites of a patient's organs and bones.
   a. CAT scans
   b. Modems
   c. Parallel processing
   d. Computer-aided design

ASSIGNMENTS

Assignment 1

Obtain two different software packages that are of the same type. For example, you might use the word processors WordStar and WordPerfect. Write a short paper comparing the two packages. Compare the features of the packages. Which package did you prefer using?

Assignment 2

Fill in the right column of the table below with the type of software that will perform the task stated in the left column.

Task	Software Needed
1. Creating pie charts and bar graphs.	
2. Writing programs in a fourth-generation language that will access records in a data base and display them in a specified manner.	
3. Designing and printing a school newspaper that includes text, artwork, and photos.	
4. Manipulating columns and rows of numeric data.	
5. Teaching people how to fly airplanes or drive cars.	
6. Creating a document that involves centering headings, changing margins, adding footnotes, and so forth.	

Chapter 17

Social Implications of Computing

CHAPTER OBJECTIVES

After studying this chapter, you should be able to:

1. Describe the development of privacy-of-information laws.
2. Explain how to use privacy-of-information laws.
3. Discuss the problems concerning privacy-of-information legislation.
4. Describe common security problems.
5. Describe controls or solutions for some common security problems.
6. Discuss why computer ethics are necessary to reduce computer crime.
7. Define public-domain software and shareware.

KEY TERMS

Computer ethics A term used to refer to the standard of moral conduct in computer use; a way in which the "spirit" of some laws are applied to computer-related activities.

Encrypted A term describing data that is translated into a secret code for security reasons.

Hacking A term used to describe the activity of computer enthusiasts who are challenged by the practice of breaking computer security measures designed to prevent unauthorized access to a particular computer system.

Piracy The unauthorized copying of a computer program written by someone else.

Public-domain software Programs unprotected by copyright law and are therefore available for free, unrestricted public use.

Shareware Programs that are distributed to the public; the author retains the copyright to the programs with the expectation that users will make donations to the author based upon the value of the program to the users.

REVIEW OF KEY TERMS

Computer _____ is a term that refers to the standard of moral conduct in
                    (1)

computer use. _____ describes the activity of computer enthusiasts who
                         (2)

attempt to break through computer security measures. Sometimes data is

_____ with a secret code to prevent unauthorized access. There have been a
            (3)

number of laws governing the access to computer systems and their data. The

_____ restricts how and when financial institutions can transfer funds. The
            (4)

_____ limits the manner in which personal data can be used by federal
            (5)

agencies. The _____ restricts agencies' access of individuals' financial
                         (6)

records and lists procedures for legally obtaining these records. The _____
                                                                (7)

outlines procedures for collection, maintenance, and access of consumer credit information.

Illegally copying software is _____. _____ software is
                                    (8)   (9)

not protected by copyright laws. _____ is protected by copyright laws but is
                                        (10)

distributed to the public in the hope that users will make donations to the author.

MULTIPLE CHOICE

1. What is the most common type of computer security problem?
    a. natural disasters
    b. computer crime
    c. employee errors and accidental destruction
    d. defective computer hardware

2. Computer ethics attempts to _____.
    a. set a standard of moral conduct for computer use
    b. limit the illegal access of data
    c. avoid the accidental destruction of data
    d. pass laws governing computer use

3. Which of the following attempted to protect consumers from inaccurate credit information?
    a. Fair Credit Reporting Act of 1970
    b. Privacy Act of 1974
    c. Right of Financial Privacy Act of 1978
    d. Electronic Transfer Act of 1980

4. Which of the following states that the government cannot access information on an individual's financial records except through a subpoena, summons, or search warrant?
    a. Fair Credit Reporting Act of 1970
    b. Privacy Act of 1974
    c. Right of Financial Privacy Act of 1978
    d. Electronic Transfer Act of 1980

5. Why has it been difficult to pass privacy legislation that governs private industry and local governments?
    a. It is not legal to control local governments.
    b. Very few people are concerned about the privacy issue.
    c. The issue of what constitutes privacy varies from region to region and industry to industry.
    d. It has not been difficult to pass such legislation.

6. Which of the following is not an objective of privacy legislation?
    a. The prevention of computer piracy.
    b. To ensure that information collected on individuals is fair and accurate.
    c. To ensure that certain records are treated as confidential.
    d. To ensure that records are not used for purposes other than those for which they were intended.

7. Shareware is software that _____.
    a. has been copyrighted but also has been made readily available in the hope that the author will receive donations from satisfied users
    b. that is copyrighted and is sold commercially
    c. that is not copyrighted and can be used without restrictions
    d. that has been stolen by a computer pirate

8. Public domain software is _____.
   a. copyrighted but can be used without restrictions
   b. copyrighted and has specified restrictions to its use
   c. not copyrighted and can be used without restrictions
   d. illegal software

9. Which of the following is an example of computer crime?
   a. An employee accidentally destroying tapes.
   b. A dissatisfied former employee destroying hardware or software.
   c. Magnetic tapes being destroyed by fire or flood.
   d. An employee forgetting to back up tapes of vital records.

10. Illegally copying software _____.
    a. is okay if you don't get caught
    b. refers to copying public-domain software
    c. encourages companies to develop more new software
    d. deprives companies and programmers of the rewards of their work

ASSIGNMENTS

Assignment 1

Visit a bank or a savings and loan that uses computers. See if you can discuss security precautions that the bank uses. Write a short report on the security precautions taken.

Assignment 2

Imagine that you are in charge of the data processing department of a large corporation. What precautions might you take to prevent accidental damage to software, hardware, and data? What precautions might you take to prevent intentional damage to software, hardware, and data? See if you can find magazine or newspaper articles that give you new ideas to add here.